D0367150

TALK
—TO—
WIN

Other Books by Dr. Lillian Glass

How to Deprogram Your Valley Girl
He Says, She Says
Say It . . . Right
World of Words

Most Perigee Books are available at special quantity discounts for bulk pur-
chases for sales promotions, premiums, fund-raising, or educational use.
Special books, or book excerpts, can also be created to fit specific needs.

For details, write: Special Markets, The Berkley Publishing Group, 200
Madison Avenue, New York, New York 10016.

TALK
—TO—
WIN

Six Steps
to a Successful
Vocal Image

LILLIAN GLASS, Ph.D.

A Perigee Book

**To an elegant gentleman and a scholar
who helped pioneer the field of speech pathology,
my mentor, Dr. H. Harlan Bloomer.**

A Perigee Book
Published by The Berkley Publishing Group
A member of Penguin Putnam Inc.
200 Madison Avenue
New York, NY 10016

Copyright © 1987 by Lillian Glass, Ph.D.
All rights reserved. This book, or parts thereof,
may not be reproduced in any form without permission.
Published simultaneously in Canada

First edition: February 1988

The Putnam Berkley World Wide Web site address is
http://www.berkley.com

Author's Note:
The cases and voices discussed throughout the book are real.
In some cases, names and identities have been changed
to preserve confidentiality.

Library of Congress Cataloging-in-Publication Data

Glass, Lillian
Talk to win.
"A Perigee book."
Includes index.
1. Oral communication.   I. Title.
P95.G54   1987   001.54′2   87-13398
ISBN 0-399-51386-8

Cover design copyright © 1987 by Mike Stromberg

Printed in the United States of America

24   25   26   27   28   29   30

Acknowledgments

I wish to thank the following people:

Adrienne Ingrum, my editor, whose wonderful insight and enthusiasm for this project have enabled me to make an even greater difference in people's lives.

Susan Grode, my agent, for her wisdom, kindness, and integrity, and for her belief in me.

Dr. Edward A. Kantor and Dr. Joseph Sugerman, two of the most highly respected ear, nose and throat physicians in the country, for their professional expertise and support in the treatment of our mutual patients.

Nina Foch for her "pearls of wisdom" and professional support.

Ana Alicia, Bob Beck, Bikram Choudhury, Joe Gallison, Melanie Griffith, Dorian Harewood, Lester Hayes, Jeffrey Kramer, Kirk Kilgore, Danitza Kingsley, Matt Lattanzi, Gloria Loring, Rob Lowe, Ronn Lucas, Dolph Lundgren, Sara Purcell, Ben Vereen, and Sela Ward not only for their participation in this book, but for their sincere friendship.

Bill Crite, Chrissy Ogden, Alan Shaffer, Rhonda Spray, and Firooz Zahidi for their photographs throughout this book. I also wish to thank Columbia and Tri-Star Pictures and Paul Jacquard and Julie Harris for helping get this book into my computer.

Finally, I wish to express my deepest love and appreciation to my parents, Abraham and Rosalee Glass, my brother and friend, Manny Glass, who always saw the potential before any one else did.

Contents

Praise for Dr. Lillian Glass's Speech Program

The best thing about working with Dr. Lillian Glass is that I became more confident. Your voice expresses how you actually feel, so you need to feel good about yourself.

What Dr. Glass writes about talking to people is similar to sports: When you know you have worked out, you have more faith in your athletic ability. Dr. Glass's program has not only helped me as a performer, but as Dolph the person in my daily life dealing with people. I can communicate better and I can judge people better. My way of carrying myself, how I animate my speech, how I carry my body, and how I breathe and relax have all gotten much better.

This program is not only great for actors but definitely great for those who must deal with people they don't know but must approach and win over.

With all the publicity I've gotten from *Rocky IV*, a number of people, like Larry King, have complimented me on my voice. One newspaper columnist said to me to just make sure I have more speaking parts in my next film because I sound terrific and am great to listen to. I attribute the rich quality of my voice and speaking skills to Dr. Glass!

—Dolph Lundgren

Dolph Lundgren *Firooz Zahedi*

Ben Vereen *You Write the Songs*

My professional growth is actual physical proof of the benefits of Dr. Glass's program. If you look at my earlier work on television and then look at my most recent work *You Write the Songs* and *Zoobalie Zoo,* you will notice the difference. Recently the *Hollywood Reporter* even said that I was a "smooth host."

On a personal level, my friends have noted my clarity, not only in the words I choose but in the points I am able to get across verbally. And for that I am thankful.

—Ben Vereen

My speech has improved by leaps and bounds. I feel very good about my speech. Thinking back four years ago, when I was interviewed on the field after a winning Super Bowl play I came in mumbling, speaking so rapidly that the words stuck, and I was embarrassed on national television.

Now I thank God and I thank Dr. Glass for the stupendous leaps and bounds that I have made in my speech. So be it!

—Lester Hayes

Lester Hayes *L.A. Raiders*

Gloria Loring *Harry Langdon*

I saw Dr. Glass because I had nodes on my vocal cords. My voice is vitally important to me on many levels. It is my profession, as well as a source of creative fulfillment. I was scared I would never be able to sing well again. In the first few minutes, she assessed my problem and comforted me by explaining what had happened and exactly how we would proceed to get my voice back to normal. She helped me understand how emotions, self-image, and stress can affect one's voice and how our vocal presentation affects the way people respond to us.

Dr. Glass's expertise made an enormous difference in my life. She can do the same for you.

—Gloria Loring

Introduction

Ever wonder how Hollywood's top stars stay on top? It's because they're always looking for new ways to be the best they can be. This includes the way they sound, and I'm often consulted to help create new images for roles actors are undertaking. For example, I worked with Dustin Hoffman as he prepared to play *Tootsie,* with Spanish singer Julio Iglesias as he rehearsed the songs for his album *To All the Girls,* and with Swedish actor Dolph Lundgren for his parts in *Rocky IV* and *Masters of the Universe.*

I teach people how to acquire and lose accents and dialects and rid themselves of bad speech habits. I also build up their confidence in their speech through the techniques described in this book. The comments of these celebrity clients are the best proof that this program works. It helped them, and it will help you.

This book is designed to help you turn people on by the way you talk. By improving the way you talk through the tones you make and through your awareness of others, you will improve your relationships with business associates, lovers, and friends.

One of the biggest fears facing Americans today is the fear of speaking with people they don't know. Shyness is our most epidemic social disease. It holds us back professionally and personally. This fear is not surprising because most of us don't speak well. We spend 80 percent of our waking hours speaking and listening, but how many of us can really do it well? Not many. But in most cases, it's not our fault. We teach our children how to read and write in school, but who teaches them how to speak? When we get older, where are we supposed to learn how to talk properly? This book is the answer.

When we send people to the moon, we talk to them via sophisticated communications systems, but we seem to be unable to talk to one another face to face.

Perhaps poor communication is why there are so many dissolutions of business and personal relationships. Look at the divorce rate. Many people divorce because they don't know how to talk to one another. Often, it is the vocal tones used, the lack of emotion in the voice, mispronunciation, monotonous drones, the inability to really listen to what the other person is trying to say that stymies us. We simply can't say what we mean.

Usually it is not what we say that affects others but how we say it. You can say "I love you" in many different ways, but if you don't say it with the right tone, you might as well not say anything at all. The same is true in business. Using varied inflections can make the difference in what you are heard to say.

Surveys show that most people can't stand the sound of their own voices. With the advent of the telephone answering machine, people have become more self-conscious about the way they sound. They often hear a voice that they don't recognize as their own. They feel frustrated and think nothing can be done about their voice. Well, here's some good news—you can change the way you sound, which can change how other people feel about you and act toward you. You are a flexible instrument, capable of making a great range of sounds. You *can* change.

If we spend billions of dollars to buy the latest fashions, to get our bodies in shape through massage and exercise, to cut and style our hair, to straighten and bond our teeth, and to nip and tuck our faces, we can certainly afford to devote a little effort to the one aspect of ourselves that is almost as important as how we look: the way we sound.

It is about time we stop underestimating the power of the sounds we make. By developing the great communication skills that I will show you in this book, you will be able to have better relationships, meet new people, have more job opportunities, and feel a lot better about yourself by improving *your total image.*

Dr. Lillian Glass
Communications Specialist

–1–
You Are Not Alone

Have you ever just met someone and found that you didn't like him or her? You didn't know what it was that bothered you, but when you gave it some more thought, you realized that it was the way the person talked.

If you have felt this way at one time or another, you are not alone. Even though you may be an open-minded person who doesn't like to judge people, you still form impressions about them.

Most of the time, when we are turned off by the way a person talks, we don't understand exactly what it is that annoys us. So, in preparing this book, I commissioned a poll by the Gallup Organization to determine how people really feel about common talking habits.

The Gallup Organization surveyed men and women from all over the United States, ranging in age from eighteen-year-olds to senior citizens, and representing all levels of income and education. People in the survey were asked about eleven frequently encountered talking habits. Did they find the habits annoying, and, if so, how much? This unique poll gives us a powerful tool for understanding exactly what it is about our speech that can cause the most problems for us. Throughout this book, I will be using these poll results to help you identify and overcome your own speaking problems.

Here are the results of the survey. The numbers are percentages of those polled.

GALLUP POLL RESULTS

	Annoys a Lot	Annoys a Little	Total Annoyed	Does Not Annoy	Don't Know
1. Interrupting while others are talking	59	29	88	11	1
2. Swearing or curse words	56	28	84	15	1
3. Mumbling or talking too softly	37	43	80	20	0
4. Talking too loudly	32	41	73	26	1
5. Monotonous, boring voice	27	46	73	26	1
6. Using filler words such as "and um," "like um," and "you know"	33	36	69	29	2
7. A nasal whine	34	33	67	29	4
8. Talking too fast	24	42	66	34	0
9. Using poor grammar or mispronouncing words	27	36	63	36	1
10. A high-pitched voice	24	37	61	37	2
11. A foreign accent or a regional dialect	5	19	24	75	1

If interrupting while others are talking annoys you, 88 percent of the people questioned agree with you. Interrupting is the number one annoying talking habit. Eighty-four percent of people questioned found swearing or cursing annoying; this was the second most annoying habit, followed by mumbling or talking too softly. A monotonous, boring voice tied with talking too loudly; 73 percent were annoyed by these speech habits.

Sixty-nine percent were annoyed by filler words, while 67 percent didn't like nasal whiners. A nasal whine, talking too fast, poor grammar and mispronounced words, and a high-pitched voice were found to be annoying by over 60 percent of the respondents. Even though the educational and socioeconomic backgrounds of the over five hundred respondents varied, certain talking habits among those surveyed were universally annoying.

The results of this poll show us that we do make judgments about people from the way they sound—no matter how unprejudiced we think we are. Oftentimes these judgments of the way a person talks can affect our relations with others. It may affect whether that person becomes our employee, banker, lawyer, doctor, lover, or even our spouse. We all make judgments about how others sound and from this decide whether they will become part of our life.

In a separate survey, I interviewed seventy-five men and women and asked them the following questions:

1. Do you feel that the way a person talks can affect his or her job opportunities?

2. Do you feel that the way a person talks can affect his or her love life?

I got a unanimous "yes" from all those questioned. These results are significant in that they verify the great impact that the way we sound has on our careers, family lives, and personal relationships.

If you judge people by the way they talk, you can be sure that people are judging *you* by the way you talk. They are making decisions about you and acting on their perceptions of you based, to a large degree, on how you speak. Most people don't pay any attention to the way they talk unless someone brings one of their annoying habits to their attention. Others hear themselves on a tape recorder and literally become disgusted with themselves. They can't believe how badly they sound. Sometimes we become more aware of our tone when directly asked about it, as in this poll. I asked people how they felt about the way they talked. An overwhelming majority of the people I questioned *disliked* the way they talked.

This information perplexes me. If we don't like the way we talk, why don't we do something about it? After all, if we don't like our noses, we can have them fixed surgically. If we don't like our bodies, we go on a diet and work out. If we don't like our hair, we change the color, shape, or style, or get some more of it through a hair transplant, monoxidil, or a toupee. If we don't like our teeth, we get braces, crowns, or dentures. But if we don't like the way we talk, why do we do nothing about it?

There seem to be three main reasons why people don't get help. First of all, they don't know that anything can be done to help the way they talk. Second, they don't know where to go for help. Finally, they don't know what it is specifically about the way they talk that bothers others.

Fortunately, something can be done about the way you talk. You no longer have to wonder about what exactly bothers you and turns people off about your talking habits. The purpose of this book is to help you improve the way you speak.

"HOW DO I TALK?" SURVEY

Don't be self-conscious or feel uncomfortable about the possibility of finding out that you have a problem. If you do find one or several problem areas, you are not alone. Millions of people have them. According to the American Speech, Language and Hearing Association in Rockville, Maryland, over 22 million people suffer from some major communication disorder. Although figures for people with minor problems have not been tabulated, I am certain that the figures would be enormous. Almost all of us can improve the way we sound.

Don't be afraid to look at yourself objectively. If you find a problem, much can be done to correct it, and correcting the problem can be an exciting thing to do. After all, didn't you marvel at the genius of the fabled Henry Higgins, who transformed a flower girl, Eliza Doolittle, into a princess in *My Fair Lady*? He gave her a renewed sense of self. By taking this survey and following the simple exercises in this book, you'll be on your way to creating a better total image.

What You Need

The first thing you must do is very carefully look at and listen to yourself. Objectively see and hear yourself the way the world perceives you.

Although they are not essential for this evaluation, a video-tape camera and recorder are great investments. Not only can you observe yourself, but you can keep a record of significant changes you make over time. If you don't have a video recorder, a full-length mirror will suffice in order to observe yourself. You definitely need a cassette or reel-to-reel tape recorder to help you analyze the way you talk.

The following questionnaire will help you focus on the way you talk. By answering these yes-or-no questions, you can learn exactly what it is about the way you talk that you don't like.

What to Do

Stand in front of the video camera and talk to yourself for about thirty seconds. Or, stand in front of a mirror and tape-record yourself. Some suggestions for what to talk about are: (1) what you have done with your life in the past, (2) what your dreams are for the future, and (3) what your personal goals are.

Be sure to look at yourself and make careful mental observations.

THE TALKING TEST

A. Body Language

YES NO

☐ ☐   Is your posture too stiff?
☐ ☐   Is your posture too loose?
☐ ☐   Is your back hunched over?
☐ ☐   Do you tilt your head down when you talk?
☐ ☐   Do you fidget when you speak?
☐ ☐   Do your hands flail around when you speak?

B. Facial Talk

Do you do any of the following while speaking:

YES NO

☐   ☐   Squint your eyes and furrow your eyebrows when you talk?

☐   ☐   Have little eye contact (eyes darting around)?

☐   ☐   Use little or no emotion in your face when you talk?

☐   ☐   Purse your lips?

C. Breathing

YES NO

☐   ☐   Do you hold a lot of tension in your neck and upper chest?

☐   ☐   Do your shoulders and upper chest move when you breathe?

☐   ☐   Do you take in a big breath and then let it all out before speaking?

☐   ☐   Do you take in a lot of little breaths when you speak?

Now turn off the video recorder or tape recorder and rewind it. As you rewind it, put your ego in your back pocket and prepare to view or listen to everything objectively. Pretend that you are analyzing someone other than yourself.

You will be observing: (A) Voice, (B) Resonance, (C) Pronunciation, and (D) Overall Communication Skills.

A. Voice

Does your voice sound:

YES NO

☐   ☐   Creaky or crackly?

☐   ☐   Strained and strangled?

☐   ☐   Harsh and choppy?

☐   ☐   Too loud?

☐   ☐   Too soft?

☐   ☐   Too high?

☐   ☐   Too low?

☐   ☐   Monotonous?

B. Resonance

YES NO

☐   ☐   Do you sound nasal and whiney (too much vibration or twang)?

☐   ☐   Do you sound denasal (stuffed up like you have a cold)?

C. Pronunciation

Do you:

YES NO

☐   ☐   Mumble?

☐   ☐   Mispronounce words?

☐   ☐   Have an accent or dialect?

☐   ☐   Have trouble with "p," "t," "k," "b," "d," and "g" consonant sounds?

☐   ☐   Have trouble with "j," "s," "z," "sh," "zh," and "ch" consonant sounds?

☐   ☐   Have trouble with "l," "w," and "r" consonant sounds?

☐   ☐   Have trouble with "m," "n," and "ng" consonant sounds?

☐   ☐   Mispronounce vowels?

☐   ☐   Have trouble distinguishing certain vowels (e.g., pin/pen)?

D. Overall Communication Skills

YES NO

☐   ☐   Do you talk too fast?

☐   ☐   Do you talk too slowly?

☐   ☐   Do you die off at the end of sentences?

☐   ☐   Do you say "um" or "like" or use fillers a lot?

☐   ☐   Do you find it difficult to carry on a conversation?

☐   ☐   Do you find it hard to meet people?

☐   ☐   Do you go on and on and on without getting to the point?

☐   ☐   Do you talk too much?

☐   ☐   Do you have a limited vocabulary?

☐   ☐   Do you curse or swear a lot?

TEST YOUR LISTENING SKILLS

Call up a friend you haven't spoken to in a long time to do this test. Tape record the conversation and play it back afterwards.

YES	NO	
☐	☐	Do you interrupt?
☐	☐	Do you constantly use "I" and talk about yourself?
☐	☐	Do you change conversations in midstream?
☐	☐	Do you sound bored and let your mind wander?

WHAT DOES ALL THIS MEAN?

Is the image you present one you do not want to project? Did you dislike what you heard when you tested your voice? If the answer to either of these questions is "yes" or if you answered "yes" to any of the questions in the test, you need some work. These questions help you become more aware of exactly what you do or don't like about the way you sound: your vocal quality, pitch, pronunciation, or resonance. Knowing exactly where your problem areas lie makes it much easier for you to work on them.

You may feel frustrated by learning how many areas you will need to work on. Don't be upset or frustrated. Get excited! You can have a better sounding image.

Continue reading this book. You will be able to identify with many of the stories. Some of the stories will remind you of yourself or of people you know. Doing the exercises in this book will help you be the best speaker you can be. It is important that you stay with it. Don't get frustrated or overwhelmed, and whatever you do, don't quit! It only takes about ten to twenty minutes to do the exercises. You can do them anytime, day or night. You can do them while you are driving your car, waiting for an appointment, or jogging, after waking up in the morning or before going to bed at night. If you do them every day you will have a great voice and sound like the person you've always wanted to be.

The program is like baking a cake; you need to mix in all the necessary ingredients (flour, water, vanilla extract, eggs, salt, butter, etc.), put it in the oven, and bake it. Similarly, you need all of the ingredients to talk correctly. You need good body and head posture, proper breath support, good voice quality, projection, proper pitch, exciting inflection, normal resonance, and exact pronunciation in order to have a great "talking image" that can affect every area of your life from your financial status to your love life.

Each one of the following chapters focuses on a particular aspect of the way you talk. Read these chapters. Do the exercises in each chapter so that you get the most out of the program. You can even incorporate some of these exercises into your everyday conversational speech.

The goal is not to make you sound like everyone else but to help you develop the best sounding image. So enjoy it!

What follows is fun and exciting! It's also easy to do and can produce amazing results in your life.

Most of my clients who have followed this program will tell you that the exercises in this book are not only easy but fun. One of the best compliments I ever received about the program was from Neil, a four-and-a-half-year-old client who told me that coming to see me and doing his speech exercises was as much fun as going to Disneyland. Neil's comment not only illustrates how enjoyable the program can be, but also shows that anyone can do it, no matter how old. My clients have ranged from age four and a half to age eighty-four and a half, and almost all of them benefited from this program.

You can do the exercises while driving to work, over the telephone when talking to friends, while you're doing housework or paperwork, even when you are in a movie theater or at a party. You can do the exercises practically anywhere, anytime, and they will help you gain the self-confidence you need to accomplish your goals. You don't have to set aside time, as you would with a physical exercise program, because the exercises take such little time and can be incorporated into your daily life. If you have had a particularly stressful day or experience, you can use the exercises to reduce stress. If you think you are going to put your foot in your mouth, many of these techniques will help stop you from doing so. If you want to be heard, many of them will help you on the spot.

RESULTS OF THE SPEECH PROGRAM

Almost all of my celebrity clients have made remarkable strides in their careers as a result of the program. While listening to a news commentary on a speech by a political candidate I worked with, I heard the reporter say that he had been following this candidate for fifteen years and had never before heard him speak with such animation. This candidate received more public support because of his new talking image.

Rob Lowe (*About Last Night*), Robert Lamm (Chicago), Melanie Griffith (*Something Wild*), Matt Lattanzi (*My Tutor*), and Don Diamont (*The Young and the Restless*) have learned to lower their voices and sound even sexier through this program. Gloria Loring (*Days of Our Lives*), Sara Purcell (*Real People*), Rita Coolidge, Bob Cummings, Bikram Choudhury (Beverly Hills yogi), and Ana Alicia (*Falcon Crest*) have used the program to get rid of vocal stress and irritation. Dolph Lundgren (*Rocky IV* and *Masters of the Universe*) and singers Sheena Easton and Ben Vereen have modified their accents through the program. Conrad Bain (*Different Strokes*), Rob Lowe (*Square Dance*), and Dolph Lundgren have used the technique to learn accents for film roles.

Director/producer Bob Rafelson uses the techniques to breathe out and release stress. Perhaps the most dramatic success story is that of Lester Hayes, five-time all-pro cornerback with the Los Angeles Raiders, who used the program in this book to help him control his stuttering.

Lester came into the N.F.L. with a severe stutter that devastated him. One year during the Super Bowl, after he caught the winning pass, the press descended on Lester. Instead of hearing flowing post-game pearls of wisdom, they heard a series of motor-like purrs, repetition of sounds, and catatonic pauses which seemed to last forever. The face of one of the best-looking players in football contorted as he uncontrollably twitched his eyes and stuck out his tongue. Millions of viewers watched him on national television. It was one of the most embarrassing moments of his life.

Lester Hayes became as dedicated to doing the exercises in

this book as he is to making winning plays on the football field. The results were dramatic. By using these techniques, he controls his stuttering, so much so that he recently talked fluently on a Raiders video, and spoke for over one-half hour without stuttering at a press conference. He now has the self-confidence to accept public speaking engagements all over the country as a spokesperson for Nike sportswear.

Recently Charlie Jones of NBC Sports interviewed Lester and introduced him as "[Having come] into the league ten years ago with a severe speech impediment, and now he's cured." ABC's Frank Gifford even said that Lester is one of the NFL players who give the best interviews and that he should be a role model for young children who may stutter.

During one interview with ABC, Lester was asked how he got his stuttering under control. His reply was, "Well, I thank God and I thank Dr. Lillian Glass."

Hearing Lester say this on national television moved me to tears. It validated the importance of my work and showed how it can literally turn people's lives around.

I should add a footnote to Lester's story. Having been a reporter for the Los Angeles ABC television affiliate KABC, I know several reporters, including sports reporters. On two separate occasions, two sports reporters half-kiddingly asked me if I could "shut Lester up because now that he can speak so well he goes on and on." I chuckled and then replied, "Good for Lester. I hope he keeps on talking as much as he wants to."

YOUR VOICE CAN MAKE YOU A WINNER, TOO

Because of the enormous success my clients have had using the program, I want to share it with you.

From years of experience in the academic world as a professor and then as a speech pathologist and communications specialist in private practice, I have seen what works over time. This program can make miracles happen for you if you practice these exercises. People who were virtually unable to speak publicly, or who hated the way they sounded, ended up loving their new talking image. People whom nobody listened to before now tell me about the compliments they receive on their voices.

The program will help you relax, be a better communicator, sustain good posture and body language, and have a more powerful, dynamic, and sexually exciting voice. It will teach you how to be a better listener, how to have good things happen to you by using more positive "self-talk," and how to develop more self-confidence. This book will also tell you how to clean up your slang and improve your vocabulary. You no longer have to suffer the prejudices that go along with not talking well. Don't worry about being a clone—sounding like everyone else. The goal is to make you sound your very best. So have fun and enjoy it!

—2—
Your Talking Image

TALKING LIKE A STAR

What do Cary Grant, Dolly Parton, Kenny Rogers, and Jane Fonda have in common?

Besides being household words, they each have a unique "talking image." The way they talk reflects the image they project to the public.

The late Cary Grant's clipped speech, hint of a British accent, and sensuous tone reflected a sexy, elegant gentleman, an image that lasted for decades.

Dolly Parton's high-pitched lilt, upward inflections, rapid speech, and charming Southern drawl reflect a bubbly, energetic person who has the stamina to write movies and songs, sing, act, start an amusement park, and still manage to make time for friends.

Kenny Rogers's deep breathy voice, punctuated by a sensuous growl from time to time, projects a strong, sensitive, and likeable man.

Jane Fonda's low-pitched voice (which gets its strength from her abdominal muscles), perfect pronunciation, and excellent pause time reflect a lady who is in control, self-assured, and poised. She comes across sincerely and with conviction.

These celebrities have talking images that accurately reflect who they are. But that's not always the case. Our talking image isn't necessarily our true image. Our voices can exude confidence when we are feeling insecure, or our voices can make us appear weak when we are actually quite capable.

Being a celebrity is no guarantee of having a good speaking voice. In fact, many have succeeded despite vocal aberrations. The media constantly bring this to the public's attention. The media focus on the shrill, high-pitched voice of Dr. Ruth Westheimer, the nasal drone of Howard Cosell, and the high-pitched, breathy voice of Michael Jackson, to name only a few.

Since we form impressions of people from how they look and from how they speak, there are certain celebrities whose voices make us form a positive impression of them and others whose tones make a negative impression.

In the second part of our exclusive Gallup poll, we asked people to judge whether they liked the way a certain celebrity talked a lot, a little, or not at all. I wanted to learn which celebrities have a favorable talking image and which celebrities have a negative one. I wanted to analyze what it was about the way a celebrity talked that we liked or disliked.

RATING THE CELEBRITIES

Rate these ten well-known people. Remember to base your opinion only on the way they talk, not whether you like or dislike their personalities or what they do.

	Not Familiar With	Like a Lot	Like a Little	Total Like	Like Not at All	No Opinion
Joan Collins	15	24	38	62	20	3
Bill Cosby	3	69	23	92	3	2
Dan Rather	10	55	28	83	5	2
Ronald Reagan	2	43	38	81	15	2
Tom Selleck	11	43	35	78	8	3

Brooke Shields	14	25	42	67	16	3
Sylvester Stallone	10	15	29	44	43	3
Barbra Streisand	7	25	43	68	23	2
Elizabeth Taylor	8	30	48	78	9	5
Barbara Walters	7	25	38	63	29	1

Which celebrities did you rate highly? Which did you rate lower? How did your answers compare with the Gallup poll results? The poll results showed that we like to listen to Bill Cosby more than any of the other celebrities; 92 percent liked the way he talks. Dan Rather came in second at 83 percent, followed by Ronald Reagan at 81 percent. Tom Selleck was fourth at 78 percent and tied with Elizabeth Taylor, who received the highest rating of any woman in the survey. Barbra Streisand followed at 68 percent, a percentage point higher than Brooke Shields at 67 percent. Next came Barbara Walters; 63 percent of the people liked the way she talks, while a close 62 percent liked Joan Collins's voice. The celebrity whose talking image was the lowest was Sylvester Stallone; only 44 percent of the respondents liked the way he sounds.

We like the way Bill Cosby sounds because he presents a talking image that is easy to listen to. He sounds relaxed and in control, yet exciting. His lower pitch adds to his credibility. He sounds likeable and trustworthy. The same is true for Dan Rather and Ronald Reagan.

Tom Selleck has a talking image that makes him likeable. His tones are not threatening and he shows enthusiasm in the way he talks.

Elizabeth Taylor's voice is low and sensuous and gives her an elegant talking image.

Even though Barbra Streisand ranked sixth, close to 70 percent of the people liked her fast-talking New York style. I'm sure if her singing voice had been rated, she would have ranked first.

Brooke Shields's score of 67 percent is still above average. This gorgeous young lady could rank even higher if she used some of the techniques in this book to make herself sound more exciting.

Although Barbara Walters ranked third to last, and was the second-lowest ranked female voice, she still rated very well; 63 percent of the people like the way she talks. Barbara Walters's talking image has been underrated because of the negative publicity about her "lisp," "r" mispronunciation, and her "Baba Wawa" image as parodied on *Saturday Night Live*. To set the record straight, Barbara Walters doesn't have a lisp or a problem with her "r"s. She has an East Coast regionalism in her speech, which many people have and which I personally find charming. Barbara Walters is a terrific talker because she sounds credible and warm and is an excellent communicator. She has done wonders for the image of women in the media.

Even though most Americans love a British accent, Joan Collins ranked second to last; only 62 percent of the people surveyed liked the way she talks. She was the lowest-ranking woman, which may indicate that most of us don't like to hear clipped and choppy, nonemotive, and harsh tones from women. It gives them a tough image. Perhaps her bitchy image on *Dynasty* reflects the talking image she projects.

The lowest-ranked celebrity was Sylvester Stallone; less than half of the people surveyed liked the way he sounds. They may have been prejudiced by his image as Rambo and Rocky, men of few words who don't sound very intelligent. In real life Sylvester Stallone is obviously highly intelligent, but his monotonous guttural sounds and mumbling don't allow him to project an accurate image of who he really is. His speech habits are disturbing; he possesses the third and fourth highest ranked annoying habits, mumbling and monotone. Perhaps if he did the exercises in this book, his voice would reflect a truer image of himself.

Even though many celebrities are hugely successful despite the way they sound, often they could be even more successful and have greater opportunities if they improved their speech.

ARE YOU WHAT YOU SPEAK?

Charles, a tall, muscular Adonis, was being eyed by almost every woman at the party. One bold woman, Joyce, noticed Charles munching hors d'oeuvres across the room and decided to introduce herself to him.

She got her courage up and headed toward the hors d'oeuvres table. She could feel her heart pounding through her chest. Her face was flushed, her breathing was shallow, her stomach was tight, and her knees were weak as she felt herself becoming physically turned on by this handsome man.

Charles looked up from his plate; his eyes met Joyce's eyes and he smiled a sensuous smile. His luscious, full lips and perfectly formed white teeth were an inviting sight.

By this time, Joyce was shivering inside. Charles then extended his strong sculptured hand toward her and said, "Hi, I'm Charles."

Immediately Joyce felt as though the entire world had fallen on her head. She was shocked back into reality. As fast as she had been turned on to Charles, she was turned off.

Why? Because Charles sounded like a wimp. Suddenly Charles was not so sexy after all. He had a high-pitched, nasal, whiny voice and did not sound like the image he projected visually.

At first Joyce thought, "What's wrong with me? Why did I get turned off?" She then realized it was because of Charles's voice. She did not like what she heard. As attracted as she was to his looks, she was repulsed by his sound.

This scenario clearly illustrates the point that our talking image, the image we project when we speak, is even more important than the physical image we project.

My doctoral research at the University of Minnesota verifies the importance of the way people sound in relation to their physical appearance. As with the party scenario with Charles and Joyce, people who were physically attractive but sounded bad were judged to be less physically attractive. By the same token, those people who were physically unattractive were judged to be more attractive if they had nice voices.

These results were verified and taken a step further during my postdoctoral research at Harbor-UCLA Medical Center. After interviewing thousands of people who were disfigured by birth defects such as dwarfism, neurofibromatosis (the Elephant Man's disease), and several other genetic disorders, I found that those people who spoke better had more success in life.

For example, one "little person" I met was a highly successful executive of a major corporation in Texas. He felt that much of his success was due to his rich, smooth, resonant, and powerful voice. What he didn't have in size, he made up for in his voice. When he spoke, people listened. The power he projected in his voice reflected the power he projected in the rest of his life. Most people forgot about his deformity, just like people did with John Merrick, the turn-of-the-century "Elephant Man," the subject of an award-winning play and film.

John Merrick was physically repulsive. The multiple tumors (neurofibromas) that covered his body made him look less than human. It wasn't until this real-life "monster" began to speak eloquently that the public changed its opinion of him. He became a hero rather than an object of disgust.

A similar case of the power that speech has over physical appearance is presented in a recent movie, *Mask*. *Mask* is the true story of a facially disfigured boy whom I happened to work with while doing my postdoctoral research at Harbor-UCLA Medical Center. This boy was teased and harassed by other children until they got to know him and talk to him. This "creature" suddenly became a sensitive, articulate person whose love touched many lives.

Although these cases are extreme, they do show how speech can be the most significant factor in making you attractive. It can determine how people want to relate to you. The image you project can determine whether a person will become your friend, lover, business associate, employer, or employee. So, your talking image can affect your personal life and your love life as well as your business life.

It can also influence how much money you make. Look at what happened to some of the athletes at the 1984 Olympics. Those Olympic stars who communicated well with the press received millions of dollars in commercial endorsements, like gymnast Mary Lou Retton. On the other hand, those athletes who weren't that communicative with the press found that their unresponsiveness cost them millions of dollars of commercial endorsements.

Studies have shown that people who speak better are perceived as being more attractive, sexy, exciting, and intelligent, and make more money. A study completed at Stanford University showed that those business graduates who had top oral communication skills earned the highest incomes. Studies have also shown that those with poor oral communication skills have fewer job opportunities and, if they are hired, receive less pay.

Other studies show that good speakers are perceived as more friendly, more successful in business, more persuasive, and more credible. Look at politicians. Much of their credibility as public figures is based on how they sound. Consider how well John F. Kennedy was received. He was perhaps our most dynamic and exciting President, largely due to his excellent abilities as a communicator.

The public didn't seem to have as much confidence in Presidents Gerald Ford and Jimmy Carter. Gerald Ford's monotone sounded boring, and Jimmy Carter's upward inflection made him sound weak. Many people were also confused by his constant smiling—which actually reflected his nervousness—even during times of crises.

On the other hand, there are politicians who are such excellent speakers that they make you believe whatever they say. Look at Ronald Reagan. He had high credibility because he sounded like he knew what he was talking about. It is obvious that all of Reagan's years in front of the camera and in front of audiences were beneficial.

THE POWER OF YOUR TALKING IMAGE

The power of your talk can change thoughts and belief systems, and can even change lives.

Listen to some of the television clergymen on Sunday. There is one gentleman who is quite dramatic as he touches people and "heals" them. He is a colorful character who wears an ill-fitting toupee that looks like a bird's nest on his head, but despite his bird's nest hairdo, the way this man talks moves people.

One evening, he claimed that he would make a deaf and

dumb child hear and speak. As a speech pathologist, I was certainly interested in his claim so I eagerly watched as he slapped the boy's ears and said, "Now he can hear!" He looked at the boy and said, "Say the word 'baby.'" In a nasal, incoherent, muffled tone the child said, "baby." Slapping and shouting, the faith healer changed the request and asked the boy to say "Jesus." The boy did not repeat the word "Jesus." Instead, he continued trying to say "baby" just as he had done twice before. It was quite obvious, at least to me, that the child still had trouble hearing and only seemed to know the word "baby."

Despite his looks and apparently false claims, some people truly buy what this evangelist is saying. His voice draws out vowel sounds in a resonant, sonorous manner, literally hypnotizing the listener. The quality captures attention and makes listeners hang on to every word. He is so entertaining and so convincing that many send their dollars in to keep him on the air.

Some of the greatest motivational speakers, like Leo Buscaglia and the Reverend Robert Schuller, captivate large audiences by the symphony of their tones. Whatever your religious attitudes or beliefs, you have to give credit to these people who can capture a vast audience with the sound of their incredibly potent voices. Millions of people tune in to hear the fluid quality of their tones, the rise and fall of their melodic pitch, and the crescendo of their vocal power followed by a wisp of breathiness. The ebb and flow of their musical communication engages ear and emotions.

Radio is another medium where the power of one's talking image is apparent. The radio talk show is one of the most powerful ways to get new ideas across. And since radio is entirely an auditory medium, the speaker's voice is what will either persuade or repel you. If the speaker's tones are exciting and powerful enough, he may sway you to his way of thinking or at least get you to be more open-minded and think about another point of view.

Martha, a strong-willed, opinionated client of mine, came into my office and said that she finally realized how important a person's voice was. After listening to Michael Jackson's (*not* the singer) talk show on KABC radio about a controversial issue she had previously made up her mind about, she was able to open her mind and look at the other side. She felt that it was Michael's soothing tone, as well as his British accent, that made her stop and actually listen.

From Michael Jackson's voice she perceived a warm, sincere, intelligent man. Because of his tone, she actually "heard" another point of view for the first time in her life and was more receptive than she had ever been in the past. Clearly, we make subconscious judgments about people, just from the way they sound, which can influence our conscious opinions.

We also make conscious judgments about people by the way they talk. A perfect example of this was aired on Dr. Toni Grant's show. Dr. Grant is a radio psychologist who is very aware of how a person's tone can reflect her psychological state.

One day, a listener called in and said, "Hi, this is Mary. I'm forty-two and I'm having trouble with my marriage."

Dr. Grant proceeded to investigate Mary's problem by asking only a few questions. Dr. Grant told her that she was very childlike in her behavior. Mary was shocked at the accuracy of Dr. Grant's diagnosis. She admitted that several people who have known her for a long time have said the same thing to her.

How did Dr. Grant know about this woman's childishness after spending only a few minutes on the telephone with her? It was not only Dr. Grant's expert psychological background but her listening abilities which cued her into Mary's childish behavior. Mary's high-pitched, whiny, nasal tone—in connection with other behavior revealed by Dr. Grant's questions— revealed immaturity.

Not everyone whose voice reflects power actually possesses that power, as shown by the TV faith healer mentioned above. A powerful talking image can be acquired. By the same token, a weak talking image can reveal inner weakness, which can be overcome by cultivating a more powerful vocal image.

PERSONALITY AND HOW YOU TALK

Galen, the Greek philosopher, was absolutely right when he said that "the voice is the mirror of the soul." The voice is an important barometer of how you're really feeling. What is going on in your head and your heart usually comes across in your voice.

You can tell if a person is in a good mood or a bad one just by the way she says "hello."

A secretary I know says she can tell what kind of a day it is going to be in the office just by the way her boss greets her in the morning.

Mike and Lisa were friends who had not spoken to each other for about six months. Yet when Lisa answered the phone and heard a male voice say, "Hello, Lisa?" she knew it was Mike even before he identified himself, and she also knew that Mike was upset just by the tone of his voice. When he told her he was getting a divorce, Lisa was hardly surprised. Mike's voice had revealed the strain, anger, and sadness that were all part of his bad news.

Anger, love, sadness, dishonesty, fear are all reflected in the sound of your voice. I meet people who think I'm a psychic because I can tell them so much about how they live their lives and how they act around other people just by hearing them talk.

One of my clients is a sixty-year-old man with a harsh and gravelly voice who was also a poor listener. He was shocked when I told him that he needed to stop trying so hard. I told him he already was a success and needed to accept that fact. I told him that his aggressiveness was a complete turn off in a man of his position and status in society. I also told him that he probably had difficulty getting along with his family.

He admitted that he did have difficulty getting along with people and that his wife, too, kept telling him to act like the success he was, not like someone trying to become a success. He also admitted having great difficulty in dealing with his children. He asked how I knew so much about him.

I learned how he got along in the world by carefully listening to what he said and how he said it. He used gravelly, attacking tones that were short, clipped, and harsh sounding, and which tended to alienate people. He used very little eye contact and kept interrupting me in his attempts to take charge of the situation. The way he sounded mirrored how he acted in the rest of his life.

Psychologists can often detect personality abnormalities just by the way a person sounds. In fact, manic depression and schizophrenia can be diagnosed largely by how a person talks. You can learn a great deal about people by paying attention to how they sound and to what they say.

Here are a few voice characteristics and related personality traits:

The Rough Graveler: People with rough, gravelly, and attacking tones often have a lot of conflict in their own lives, including a lot of difficulty getting along with people. These people beat up their vocal cords by using attacking sounds that can harm their voices. They often harm interpersonal relations, as well, by their unpleasant tones. Even when they are not upset they sound upset. They tend to abuse the person they are talking to through a barrage of crackles and choppy tones which are hard to listen to.

The Baby Woman: An inappropriately high-pitched voice (a forty-two-year-old woman sounding like a twelve-year-old) may reveal an immature person who retains many childish characteristics and behavior patterns. I see many women who put on this unappealing "little girl" act. They sound cute and breathy and have lots of head movements and body mannerisms. They think they are being feminine and charming but they are being ridiculous. What worked at ten doesn't work at fifty.

The Bore: If the voice is monotonous and boring the person may have some inner problems expressing emotion or getting emotionally close to others. Such people may also be apathetic or lethargic. They usually don't talk much. Getting them to talk is like pulling teeth. They are people of few words and feel that if they don't talk much, people will have less to judge them on. What they don't realize is that they are judged negatively just because they clam up. They are so frustrating to talk to that others usually give up.

The Fog Horn: People who talk too loud, providing they have no hearing problem, may have ego problems. They have a need to be noticed. There is a great need for attention and an unawareness of others around them. You have most likely heard these people at a public place, usually when you're on vacation. You might even find such people at a quiet restaurant where you're jolted by a loud, obnoxious person hogging the sound waves while you're engaged in intimate conversation. The term "ugly American" may have been developed because of such people.

The Wimp: A too-soft voice, swallowing one's words, or dying-off at the end of sentences may signal insecurity and low self-esteem. The Wimp seems to have little self-confidence and to be timid in expressing himself. He may feel that what he says isn't that important, so he whimpers out his sounds.

The Motor Mouth: Talking too fast may signal insecurity as well as impatience. Getting everything out as quickly as possible may diminish the importance of what is being said. Usually you can't understand these people. When you ask them to repeat what they said, they get irritated with you, which makes them talk even faster, which makes you ask them to repeat themselves again, which leaves the two of you frustrated.

These generalizations are based on my years of observation of personality traits and the role that the voice plays in personality characteristics. Think of people you know who have these characteristics. In most cases, the descriptions will fit their personality traits accurately.

FALSE IMPRESSIONS

Even though your tones may reveal your true personality, it is entirely possible that your tones may reflect a false talking image as they did with the "Gravelling Grandmother."

Dorothy, a grandmother who adores her grandchildren, brings them gifts and candy every time she visits them. But she can't understand why they like their other grandmother better.

Her harsh, gravelly, low voice quality and rapid speech rate give her a battle-ax image that alienates her not only from her grandchildren but from anybody she meets. It's not until people get to know her that they realize she is a sweet, friendly, and caring woman.

Another example of a voice and manner that can give the wrong impression is seen in the "Irritating Countess."

Ilona, the beautiful forty-five-year-old wife of a socially prominent businessman, dresses like a countess, smells great, looks stunning, and has exquisite posture and a regal walk. However, when you talk to her, you get a different picture.

She talks loud, fast, breathlessly, with irritating body language, flailing her arms all over the place as she speaks. Her voice is harsh. She feels that she always has to be "on." She doesn't listen. She finds that she has few friends.

Whenever she is at a business function with her husband, she doesn't feel accepted. She notices that people are initially drawn to her and then are turned off. Party and dinner invitations are rarely reciprocated. People generally are upset by Ilona because the talking image she gives is incongruous with the initial image they had of her.

Maryanne is a forty-five-year-old female with a voice like a machine gun. She talks so fast that the message that comes across says, "Stay away from me. Don't touch me." She wonders why nobody asks her out.

She was divorced twice; every relationship she ever had was a failure. Her rapid attacking tones made her sound biting, tart, and acrid. Most people were afraid of her and uncomfortable around her. Besides, they couldn't understand what she was saying half the time because she talked so fast.

Tamara, a thirty-eight-year-old housewife and mother of three, had a high-pitched, little-girl voice. She hated her relationship with her husband; she felt that he was controlling and domineering and treated her like one of the children. This was not surprising because she spoke like one of the children.

Debbie was a Harvard law student who was tops in her class, graduating with highest honors. However, she lost out on many positions during interviews with law firms.

One interviewer boldly told her that if he hadn't looked at

her academic records he would have thought she was mentally retarded. She was devastated to hear this from an interviewer at a prestigious law firm.

But his comment didn't surprise her because people had pointed this out to her in the past. She would be at a social function and people would ignore her or quickly leave after their introduction when they heard her speak.

She had a little girl, high-pitched, breathy, babyish voice and used a lot of "like ums" throughout her speech. Because she was a Californian, many thought she was just a Valley Girl. Little did they know what a brilliant mind lurked under her Valspeech.

Gary is a resident in anesthesiology who was very good at the technicalities of his profession. He proved this when he received a very high score on the written part of his qualifying examinations.

Despite his knowledge, he couldn't become a practicing anesthesiologist because he failed the oral portion of his National Board examinations three times. He never maintained eye contact with his examiners, mumbled, died off at the end of sentences, and spoke in a gloomy monotone. In essence he sounded like a cadaver, a dead body. His bedside manner certainly didn't instill a lot of confidence in his patients either.

Jeffrey, a soft spoken divorcé, seemed to reflect the problem, made comical by Rodney Dangerfield, of not getting any respect. He had poor eye contact and would literally fade off at the end of sentences. He hardly opened his mouth or moved his lips when he spoke. Nobody ever seemed to pay any attention to what he had to say, not even his daughters.

Ted was a seventeen-year-old computer whiz kid. He spoke so softly that you could hardly hear him. He didn't make any eye contact. He was so frustrated whenever anyone asked him to speak up that he rarely spoke. He was petrified about attending a college mixer because he was afraid to talk. He knew that if he spoke, people would ask him to speak up, so he refused to attend.

CHANGING YOUR TALKING IMAGE

In all of these cases, the way people sounded gave such a bad impression that it limited their lives. In most of the cases, the speakers' tones didn't reflect who they really were. In other cases, their tones reflected such a terrible talking image that few cared to find out who they really were. If these people could change the way they talked, they would change how people treated them. Every one of these people was able to modify his or her speech patterns to project a better talking image. The changes in their lives were remarkable.

As Dorothy, the grandmother, modified her harsh, gravelly voice, she found not only her grandchildren to be more receptive, but her daughter as well. In fact, her daughter called to thank me for the change in her mother, and only wished her mother had learned the techniques in this book and changed her talking image years ago.

Ilona the Irritating Countess learned to speak in flowing tones, modulate her loudness, and become a better listener. In doing so, she has discovered a new world of friends. She gets invited to more parties and finds that people tend to stick around longer than they ever have before.

When Maryanne, the fast-talking forty-five-year-old, learned to slow down, she met several men who wanted to date her. She also learned to become a better listener.

When Tamara, the thirty-eight-year-old housewife learned to speak like a woman in low flowing tones and not in her high-pitched squeak, her entire relationship with her husband changed. He now treats her like the sexy woman she is.

The brilliant Valley Girl's speech got deprogrammed as she learned to control her "like ums" and "ums" and lower her high-pitched, breathy voice. This resulted in getting her a job in a prestigious law firm.

By livening up his voice, and adding some warmth and excitement, Gary, the anesthesiology resident, passed his oral examination and has developed such a good bedside manner that many of the doctors in the hospital request him as the anesthesiologist on their surgery cases.

Jeffrey, the "I don't get any respect" divorcé, learned to project his voice so well that he shocked his daughters. Once, when his daughters were bickering in the car, he squeezed his abdominal muscles and projected his voice loudly, yelling, "Stop it right now!" Both girls were so shocked that they started to cry. Old Dad suddenly felt a renewed sense of power, power over himself that he had had all of his life, only he didn't know it.

Ted, the meek-talking computer whiz kid, learned to use the techniques in this book to help him to control his shyness as well as his vocal projection. Today he is a coxswain on the rowing team at an Ivy League university and has more friends than he ever dreamed he would have. This is due to his renewed self-confidence, which he projects in his voice and in his body language.

Ted's parents also can't get over the change in his attitude since he gained control over his speaking. They were even thrilled with his behavior at the dinner table. Before, he would look down at his food and answer questions in one-word, curt responses. Today, he looks into your eyes, talks to you, and is the one asking questions.

Ever since Demosthenes, who, in ancient Greece, placed pebbles in his mouth to stop his stuttering, a multitude of famous and not-so-famous people have had to overcome physical and psychological limitations in order to improve the way they sounded. Many have gone on to accomplish great things with their lives. These people did whatever it took to rebuild their talking images.

Sometimes the talking image that worked in the past is no longer appropriate as we grow and change. But you don't have to live with the old image. You can change your talking image if it doesn't reflect who you presently are. You can become the person you want to be.

Follow the exercises in each of the chapters and you will develop a terrific talking image.

YOUR TALKING IMAGE AND YOUR SOCIAL LIFE

A poor speaking voice can ruin your social life. The telephone has become a powerful tool for socializing, but, with the advent of the answering machine, more and more people are discovering how awful they sound over the phone. If you sound good over the phone, your voice can enhance your social life. Don't be inhibited by the telephone. Certainly it's a mechanical barrier but, in reality, it's only a transmitter and amplifier. To make talking on the phone more comfortable, you need to let yourself go and pretend that there is a warm receptive person on the other end of the line who wants to talk to you.

There are also telephone dating services where men and

Rob Lowe, in a scene from *About Last Night* (Tri-Star), listens to someone over the telephone. The sound of your voice can affect how the listener reacts toward you both professionally and socially. *Courtesy Tri-Star Pictures, Inc., © 1986*

women can record their singles advertisements, which repeat twelve times each hour. The better they sound, the better their chance of getting a date.

Video dating services have been springing up all across the country, clearly showing the effect that speech and appearance have on whether a person is selected for a date or not. These dating services illustrate how much more important a person's talking image is than looks alone. Frequently someone may be attracted to a person's photograph, but when that person is viewed on videotape, he or she is a turn off. What turns others off is sound or body language or posture.

Peter, a single client who used a video dating service, found that after watching their videotapes he was only attracted to one in four women whose photos he had chosen. He said that the thing that turned him off the most was the way several of these women carried themselves—their poor posture, fidgeting, stiffness, and, of course, the sound of their voices.

A sad commentary, but there is hope. By improving their talking images people can improve their social lives, as a client of mine did.

Arthur, a widower, wanted to get back into the dating scene but was discouraged by the number of rejections he got at a video dating service. It was his outdated appearance and manner of speech that were the probable causes. He updated his wardrobe and hairstyle and improved his talking image, his poor head posture, hunched back, and constant lip pursing. He used the techniques in this book to help him with his speech.

Three months later he returned to the video dating service to make a new tape. He found that the response to him was much more favorable. For the first time, he was selected as a date by several women, one of whom he married.

Yes, it can happen to you too! Even though all of these stories sound promising, many of you skeptics may be saying to yourselves, "How does this apply to me? Do you mean that if I clean up my so-called talking image, I'll get married or make more money or have a better job?"

My answer is *yes*, you will have a better chance to do so. Read on and let's begin making your life more exciting!

—3—
Face and Body Languages

Remember Dustin Hoffman in *Tootsie?* As Dorothy, the woman, his hands were close to his body. His movements were small and fluid; took up less room. When he portrayed Michael Dorsey, his gestures were more open, massive, away from his body, and he took up more room.

I was one of the first people to help Dustin prepare for *Tootsie.* I helped him to delineate the differences in the way men and women use their bodies to communicate.

Even though there are differences between male and female body language, some rules for having good body language apply to everyone. This chapter will not concentrate on what particular body movements mean. By now, most of us have seen or read books or articles on that subject, such as *Body Language* by Julius Fast, *Love Signals* by David Givens, or *Signals* by Allan Pease. So we know that if someone crosses his arms, he seems to be closing off contact. Or if someone places the tips of his fingers together, "steepled" under his chin, he may appear important.

This chapter focuses on how you can develop excellent body and head posture, which can help you present yourself in a better way. Through a series of exercises, you will learn to reduce tension in your neck and shoulders and appear more

Dustin Hoffman in *Tootsie* **used typically feminine body and face language to express himself as a female.** *Courtesy Columbia Pictures, copyright 1982. All rights reserved.*

confident. You will learn what to do with your hands when you speak, the importance of good posture, the necessity of a strong handshake, and the effects of touching other people when you talk to them. You will learn how to become more facially animated and how to develop better eye contact when you speak and when you listen. The exercises will help you make people respond more favorably toward you.

STAND TALL/SIT UP STRAIGHT

"Stand up straight!" "Stop walking with your shoulders hunched!" "Keep your head up!" Most of us had these reprimands barked at us by our parents while we were growing up. At the time, we wished they would leave us alone and stop badgering us about such trivial things as the way we walked or stood. Some of us listened and were conditioned to have good posture. Others of us ignored the reprimands, continued to slouch, and carried this bad habit into adulthood.

Your posture is one of the first things people look at. It allows people to determine how confident you are and how they will treat you initially. If you don't have enough self-respect to stand up straight, others may feel that they don't need to give you that much respect either. Look at how the characters that Woody Allen portrays in his movies are treated, and look at what their posture says about them. His hunched-over, head-hanging, slouched character says, "I'm an underdog. I have no self-confidence. I'm a nerd. Nobody respects me."

People do make judgments based on our posture. When one hundred people were shown photographs of people with poor posture (head down, shoulders rounded, stomach out) and photographs of people with good posture (head up, shoulders back), the people with poor posture were consistently judged to be less popular, less exciting, less ambitious, less friendly, and less intelligent than their counterparts with good posture. This was the case for both sitting and standing posture.

Your posture is the key to communicating your image. A posture that is too stiff communicates uptightness, while a posture that is too loose communicates sloppiness and carelessness. A hunched over back and neck that is too far forward shows a lack of confidence and self-respect.

Oftentimes initial judgments people make about us on the basis of our posture determine how they will treat us. Donald is a thirty-six-year-old executive who just got promoted into a high-level position in his company. He had to work with people he had never worked with before. After two months on the job, he felt that he had difficulty being treated like a leader by his

employees. He came to see me for a consultation about his
image. When I saw his terrible posture, with rounded shoulders
and hanging head and protruding belly, I could see why his
employees had a difficult time taking Donald seriously and
treating him with the respect that he deserved. His posture
screamed, "I have no self-respect, so you don't have to respect
me either."

After working on his posture by doing the exercises in this
book, Donald improved his posture dramatically. He learned
to walk, stand, and sit with his back straight, his shoulders back,
and his head up. It gave him more confidence, which he projected to his employees. He began to notice that they treated
him with more respect. He especially saw the effect that his
newfound posture had when he met people for the first time:
he observed that their initial attitudes toward him were much
more positive.

When Sheila was thirteen she developed large breasts, which
made her an object of desire for everyone in her class. The
other girls all hoped to have breasts like Sheila's, and the boys
teased her about them. With all this attention directed toward
her breasts, Sheila became terribly self-conscious and began to
hide them by rounding out her shoulders so that they would
appear to be flatter. This seemed to work; the teasing dwindled.
Although Sheila believed that her new posture was responsible,
the teasing may have stopped because as her peers grew more
mature their own breasts developed. Sheila's breasts were no
longer the object of attention.

Sheila's troubles may have been delayed during her teens
but, when she reached her twenties, her habit of rounding her
shoulders to hide her breasts resulted in terrible posture and
poor self-esteem. Because her breasts seemed to be objects of
her disdain, she underwent breast-reduction surgery but still
didn't like how she looked. When she came to see me to work
on her image, the first thing we did was develop her posture.

Because her shoulder and neck muscles were so tight from
years of hunching over, she did hundreds of shoulder rolls and
head rolls. These exercises helped her get rid of all of her
tension. They worked beautifully for Sheila, and she has an

excellent posture today. Whenever she lapses back into her old habits, she does the Head Roll and Shoulder Roll exercises and is able to regain her new posture and feel more confident.

Sheila's story is quite common. So many women develop poor posture because, as teenagers, they do not have the self-esteem it takes to carry themselves properly as they develop breasts.

When you develop good posture you can change the way you feel about yourself. Sitting erect instead of slumping and standing straight as though you were an important person can help you feel more important and help turn negative feelings about yourself into positive ones. In order to keep good posture, you need to practice "mindfulness." This concept was developed in Eastern thought and refers to a constant awareness. To help you control your body language, pretend that you have a third eye on your middle finger that constantly observes you. This will help you maintain an objective awareness of your posture and body movements at all times so that you will be conscious of using good posture until it becomes a habit.

Posture Exercises

1. One of the best techniques for examining your posture is to look in the mirror or, if you have access to a video recorder, to record yourself on videotape. Observe how you stand and how you sit. Are your shoulders rounded? Is your stomach pouched out when you stand or when you sit? Are your legs sprawled out? Are your chest and shoulders at the same level? Is your chin well above your shoulders?

2. For good standing posture, stand up straight and tighten your buttocks. Next, pretend that you have a satin rope running straight from the top of your head to the base of your spine. Make sure that your arms are at your sides. If you are hunched over or too far back, the imaginary rope will not be parallel to the base of your spine. Make sure this imaginary rope is straight at all times. Your posture will be straight.

3. To have good posture when sitting down, it is important to place your buttocks all the way at the back of the chair first. Your back will automatically become straight as it rests against

the back of the chair. If you sit down and then slide back, you will have more of a tendency to slouch.

4. Shoulder Rolls

The Shoulder Roll Exercises will help you to release tension from your neck and shoulder muscles. They will also train you to develop good posture as you learn to recognize the sensation of keeping your shoulders back.

A. First rotate the right shoulder forward and keep it in position for three seconds.

B. Rotate the left shoulder forward and keep it there for three seconds so that both of your shoulders are forward.

C. Now rotate the right shoulder back and keep it in position for three seconds.

D. Rotate the left shoulder back and maintain that position for three seconds so that both shoulders are back.

E. Repeat this exercise ten times.

5. Both-Shoulder Rolls

Rotate both shoulders forward and hold for three seconds, and then move both shoulders back for three seconds. Do this ten times. When the shoulders are both rotated backwards, they are in proper position for maintaining good posture. *Firooz Zahedi*

HEADS UP

Remember watching the old Laurel and Hardy movies? Whenever Ollie yelled at Stanley, Stanley would bow his head down in shame and make a comical expression indicating his embarrassment over the particular "mess I got us into this time."

So many of us walk around with our heads in that bowed, shameful position when we have nothing to be ashamed about. This head bow negatively influences our self-image.

Dr. Barry is a successful eye surgeon who developed a new surgical technique for improving vision so that people would not need to wear glasses. After his first television appearance, a close friend was honest enough to tell him to come to me for some on-camera coaching before he did another television talk show. When Dr. Barry and I watched the videotape of his TV interview, he was amazed at how he constantly bowed his head when he spoke. His eyes were cast downward and when he did look up, his head was still bowed. This made him appear unsure of himself and tentative. It made the viewer question the doctor's confidence in his own abilities. Dr. Barry felt that he looked "eerie and monstrous." When he jokingly said, "I would never trust that man," I knew he got the message. Even though he was a fine physician and an expert in his field, his poor head posture projected a different image. He now understood why he did not receive many calls from viewers after the program aired.

The public response changed dramatically the next time he was on television. He had learned to monitor his head posture. He received so many calls for appointments from new clients that his practice boomed overnight.

Head Posture Exercises

Pretend that you have an imaginary satin cord hooked to the crown of your head. Imagine the cord being gently pulled up, bringing your head up along with it. Use the mindfulness technique described earlier to remain aware of your head position throughout the course of the day.

1. Head rolls are excellent ways to get rid of tension in your

Head Posture: Actor Joe Gallison shows poor head posture, which so many people are guilty of. By pretending that there is a satin cord pulling the head up, we can maintain good head posture. *Alan Shaffer.*

head and neck region. (A) Very slowly rotate your head to the right. Feel all the muscles stretching in your neck as you rotate it inch by inch. (B) Now rotate the head to the back very slowly and gently. (C) Keep rotating the head around to the left. Don't be surprised if you hear some of the bones in your neck cracking. It means that you were tense and really needed to do this exercise. (D) Continuing on, rotate the head downward, feeling all the muscles stretch. Do this gently and slowly five times to the right. (E) Do the exercise five more times but in the opposite direction. Begin by rotating the head to the left, then back, to the right, and then to the front. This exercise will also help you to become more aware of your neck in relation to your head position and posture.

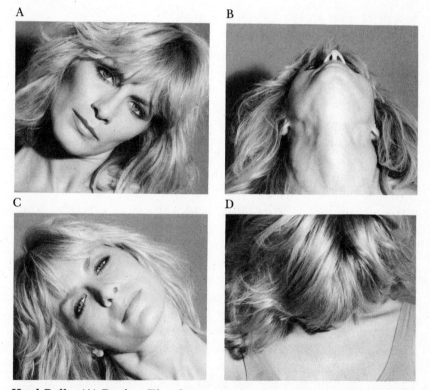

Head Rolls: (A) **Danitza Kingsley rotates her head to the right,** (B) **to the back,** (C) **to the left and** (D) **down. This process can also be reversed starting at the left.** *Bill Crite*

2. Another exercise that you can do when you are alone at home or when you are talking with friends or family, or even when you are driving in your car, is wearing a cervical collar. The foam rubber kind, which you can get in any drugstore, has a velcro back that is light weight and easy to manipulate. Wearing the collar five to ten minutes a day can help you become more aware of your head dropping downward. Every time you drop your head it will feel uncomfortable. You will know that you have broken the habit of poor head posture when you don't even realize that you are wearing the collar.

3. Once again, you need to practice the mindfulness technique so that having good head posture becomes a habit.

WATCH THOSE FLAILING ARMS

The way you use your arms and hands when communicating can turn people on or off. People who fold their arms across their chest when they talk are more alienating than those who rest their hands on their laps. A study done by Jimmi Harigan of the University of Cincinnati and Robert Rosenthal of Harvard University, showed that people think a physician has greater rapport with patients when he has a more open arm and hand position. The patients felt that the physician was more accessible to them.

Using the hands when you speak can be an excellent communication technique because your hands can help express an idea or emphasize a thought. However, too much arm or hand movement can be a turn-off, so it is important to be careful of how often you gesture when you speak.

Arms and hands that flail around when you speak and hands that are constantly fidgeting are severe enough distractions that they diminish your total image. They communicate a sense of discomfort and uneasiness to the listener, who becomes less patient with you and feels more anxious around you. The arm-flailer may even become a laughing stock, as Monica did.

Monica is a thirty-eight-year-old account executive. Her duties include giving presentations in front of both large and small groups. One day while walking past a colleague's office, she overheard her colleagues talking about her. She heard someone say, "I'll bet Monica couldn't utter a word if someone tied her hands behind her back." She then heard someone else snicker and reply, "Yeah, doesn't she look like a wild chicken flapping in the wind?" and then both laughed.

Monica was devastated by what she overheard. She worked hard at her job. She spent hours preparing for her talks, apparently only to be ridiculed by her peers. She had no idea that she "flapped her arms like a chicken" when she spoke. Luckily, someone in the company came up with the brilliant idea of videotaping presentations so that the company could develop a tape library and eliminate the need for repetitive presentations. She got hold of her videotape for a private viewing. After looking at the tape she started to cry. She couldn't believe what she saw. She did indeed look like a flapping chicken. Her colleagues were absolutely right. She even wondered if she could speak if her hands were tied. Even though watching herself on videotape was one of the most painful things Monica had ever done, she learned a tremendous amount from doing it. She also used the mindfulness technique to help her control her extraneous arm and hand gestures.

Mindfulness Exercises for Gesturing

1. If you can videotape yourself when you are talking to a close friend or while you are giving a presentation, you can learn much about yourself, as Monica did.

2. Be mindful of how much gesturing you are doing and try to gesture only when emphasizing important points.

3. Be sure to keep your hands on your lap when you are sitting or at your sides when you are standing.

4. Try to keep your fingers relaxed. Doing so will often relax your hands and arms and even the rest of your body.

5. If you are still at a loss about what to do with your arms and hands, you may want to use Prince Charles's and Princess Di's approach. Keep your hands clasped in back of you when you walk. Doing this suggests a sense of control, security, and

self-assurance. After all, if it makes the future king and queen feel more secure and in control when they are walking around in public, it can certainly do the same for you.

YOUR HANDSHAKE SAYS A LOT

You can tell a lot about people by the way they shake hands. A handshake can not only reveal a lot about you, but in some cases, your handshake can reflect how you actually feel about the person you are shaking hands with. The looser and less firm your handshake is, the less comfortable you make the other person feel. On the other hand, too tight a grip may indicate your inner aggression toward that person or your desire to be the dominant one in the relationship. A firm handshake of about three seconds indicates confidence and self-assuredness, especially when you meet someone for the first time.

If you want to convey warmth and show that you really like the other person, you may want to use the double handshake— put your left hand on top of the other person's right while you shake hands.

I have often come across large men who have wimpy hand-shakes because they are afraid of intimidating the other person. In their attempt to come across as gentle and nonthreatening, they come across as weak. The people they are shaking hands with are often taken aback by this and begin to change their initial impression of them. Even if you are not feeling comfortable when you first meet people, remember that they may feel the same way you do. So you can make them feel more comfortable by securing a firmer handshake. Try this the next time you meet someone new. Use a firmer handshake for three seconds. If you really like the person, put your left hand over your right, cupping his or her hand in both of yours. Then watch the positive response you get.

REACH OUT AND TOUCH

We live in a society where most of us are afraid to touch one another. As children we didn't think twice about touching others to indicate how we felt about them. Unfortunately, as we grow up we tend to touch less and less. Most people want to be touched. The effect that touching has on another person is extremely important in terms of the underlying impressions you can make on others.

In a university study, students were either touched or not touched by the library clerk in the process of checking out books. They were then asked to participate in an evaluation of library personnel and facilities. The results showed that students who were touched rated the clerks more positively than those who were not. Studies also show that the greater the amount of touch, the more positive the reaction.

It is important to touch other people when you talk to them because touching is one of the best ways to cement your communication experience with the other person. A pat on the back or a touch of the arm not only help underscore important points, but helps break down barriers.

Ana Alicia of *Falcon Crest* is one of my dearest friends. She is nothing like Melissa Gioberti, the villainess she portrays in the popular television series. She expresses herself warmly and as a result communicates very well. After five minutes of talking to her you feel that you have known her all your life. Ana Alicia touches people a lot when she talks to them. She is open and is not afraid to touch people to let them know how she feels about them.

Touching is vital for our human survival. We all need to be touched. Don't be afraid to touch someone throughout your conversation because sometimes a touch can communicate more than a thousand words. Touching can also be the very thing the other person was longing for. It may make the difference between becoming a friend and remaining an acquaintance.

Don't feel rejected if you reach out and touch someone and you are met with a frown or find her stiffening up or backing away from you. Instead, be sensitive if she recoils from you. The person may not feel comfortable around you so you may want to back off. By touching the person, you got a more realistic indication of their reaction toward you. If the person recoils, keep in mind that it may have absolutely nothing to do with you. Some people may not be used to being touched by others and may feel uncomfortable when touched. Others may not like to be touched because of cultural background. Studies have shown that certain cultures touch less than others. A study by British scholar S. M. Jourard found that South Americans and the French touch one another more than Americans or the English do. In the business world it is often inappropriate for men and women to touch one another because sexual harassment has become an important concern. Use your judgment in such matters.

Despite these factors, most people hunger to be touched, as Ashley Montagu points out in his book *Touching*. So don't be afraid to take a chance and touch people when you talk to them. Remember the theme song, "Reach Out And Touch (Somebody's Hand)," by Nickolas Ashford and Valerie Simpson, used in the opening ceremonies of the 1984 Summer Olympics? What great advice! We always need to keep it in mind. If we reach out and make the first move, we may be pleasantly surprised at what we get back.

FACE TALK

The facial expressions you use when you talk are important because they create a distinct first impression about you.

A team of psychologists and political analysts at Dartmouth found that Ronald Reagan may have had an early advantage in his 1980 campaign because the emotional intensity and diversity of his facial expressions created a positive first impression. Whether or not they agreed with his political views, all the subjects in the study who watched videotapes of his varied emotions showed physiological changes in their skin and in their heart rates. The researchers also found that those who watched Reagan helped sway those who had not yet made up their minds to support him.

This interesting research clearly demonstrates the effect that a person's facial expression can have on the way he is perceived by others, and in turn how others react to him.

On the other hand, if you do not use the appropriate facial expression when you speak you may be misrepresenting yourself.

If you have too much tension in your facial muscles when you speak, you may appear to be angry or uptight when in reality you are not. This was the case with Stephanie. Throughout her adult life, she has repeatedly heard comments like this: "I thought you were so bitchy before I got to know you" or "You are so much nicer than I thought." Because Stephanie got so sick of hearing these comments, she came to me to help her get rid of her tense facial expressions when she talked.

What Stephanie was doing was giving out mixed messages. The tightness in her face, her furrowed forehead and knitted brow, intense eye contact and pinched, pursed lips gave the impression that she was a mean person.

By learning how to progressively relax her facial muscles and becoming mindful of her facial expression at all times, Stephanie was able to change people's initial reactions toward her. By doing the facial and facial animation exercises that follow, she learned to control her facial muscles and synchronize her emotions with the appropriate facial responses. After becoming able to control her facial animation, Stephanie felt that she had overcome the biggest obstacle in her life. She gained more self-confidence than she ever had before.

Sometimes when you are listening intently to what someone is saying, you listen so intently that you appear to be scowling and frowning. This in turn may inhibit their opening up to you as they may perceive that you are judging them or disapproving of them when you are not; you are merely listening intently.

Therefore, it is essential to be mindful whenever you are listening. Keep your eyes open when you listen and don't furrow your brow.

Facial Relaxation Exercises

1. If your facial muscles are tense in certain areas (furrowed forehead, pursed lips, tense jaw), every hour or so make yourself aware of what parts of your face are feeling tense. Close

Facial Vacation: Actress Sela Ward takes a facial vacation by closing her eyes and relaxing her forehead, eyes, nose, cheeks, lips, jaw, ears, and neck and visualizing herself relaxing on a far away island. *Alan Shaffer*

your eyes and take a minivacation for fifteen seconds. Picture yourself in your fantasy environment, relaxed and calm. Think great thoughts!

2. Keeping your eyes closed, imagine all tension leaving your forehead, eyes, nose, cheeks, upper and lower lips, jaw, ears, and neck. Open your eyes and look at yourself in the mirror. See a beautifully relaxed face.

3. It's not a bad idea to keep a mirror near your desk or on a wall across from your desk so you can see how you come across. It will help you to monitor your body, head, and facial movements throughout the day.

4. Having a friend or family member remind you when you are committing one of your bad facial habits can also be very helpful. Just make sure you tell them to point it out subtly and positively, not with harassment or negativity.

ANIMATE—DON'T ALIENATE

Approximately 75 percent of our nonverbal communication is done with our face. It is essential that we learn to use our facial muscles to express ourselves accurately.

Facial animation is an essential part of our language as Charles Darwin pointed out as early as 1872. Just as inappropriate facial animation can confuse people and become a "turn off," using too little facial expression can turn people off as well. Many people, especially businessmen, are trained to use a poker face in doing business so that they don't let the other party know what they are thinking or feeling. This poker face technique is designed to keep the other party off guard.

Personally, I don't think that this is a very comfortable way to do business. It adds to the already stressful situation and often clouds the issues that need to be dealt with openly and honestly. The poker face technique may become dangerous when carried over to personal interactions. This is commonly referred to as game playing—not showing how you really feel about the other person. If we want to have more honest and meaningful relationships with others, we need to stop holding back and start wearing our emotions on our faces. We have to stop being afraid of exposing our true selves. Most of the time it turns out to be better than our game playing, poker-faced selves.

Dr. Paul Ekman of the University of California at San Francisco has made a career of studying facial expression and facial animation. He has mapped out a technique for coding facial expressions called FACS, Facial Action Coding System, based on the role of the facial muscles in expressing different emotions. His research indicates that there are seven emotion expressions that are universal. They are sadness, happiness, anger, interest, fear, contempt, and surprise.

Using a modified version of Dr. Ekman's technique, adding the emotions of love, doubt, compassion, and boredom and deleting interest, I have devised an exercise which can help you to project more accurate facial expressions when you speak and listen.

Facial Animation Exercise

Look at each of the ten photographs of actor Jeffrey Kramer (*Jaws III*). Act out the emotion it illustrates by using the appropriate facial muscles. Practice this exercise in front of a mirror, making sure you believe the emotion you are portraying.

Sadness
- Raise your eyebrows.
- Wrinkle your forehead.
- Depress your lower lip.

Surprise
- Raise your eyebrows.
- Slightly raise your upper eyelids.
- Open your mouth.

Anger
- Lower your eyebrows.
- Stare hard.
- Raise your lips.
- Open your mouth.

Happiness
  • Raise your cheeks.
  • Part your lips.
  • Drop your jaw.
  • Smile.

Fear
  • Raise your eyebrows.
  • Raise your upper eyelids.
  • Stretch your lips.
  • Open your mouth.

Disgust
  • Raise your upper lip.
  • Wrinkle your nose.
  • Open your mouth.
  • Raise your chin.

Compassion and Sympathy
  • Lower your head.
  • Tighten your lips.
  • Lower your eyes.

Love
- Smile slightly.
- Flare your nostrils.
- Slightly protrude your
  lower lip.

Doubt
- Lower your head.
- Raise your eyebrows.

Boredom
- Stare vacantly.
- Slightly shift your jaw to
  one side.
- Slightly flare your nos-
  trils.

Photos by Bill Crite

THE EYES HAVE IT

Have you ever been to a party or at a club where the person you are talking to is constantly glancing about the room to see who else is there? You begin to feel uncomfortable. You ask yourself, "Does this person really care about what I have to say?" Feeling rejected, you may find yourself glancing about the room as well, as your defenses go up. This is reflected in your superficial conversation and your abrupt exit. Even though you agree to exchange phone numbers, you couldn't care less if that person ever calls you. You are on the defensive and are left with a sour taste in your mouth, thinking that that was one of the rudest people you have ever met because he didn't bother to look into your eyes when you were talking.

This scenario is a common and disheartening one. Most of the time, people don't mean to be rude. Often they don't even realize what they are doing.

It is hard to focus all of your attention on one person when there is a lot going on around you. You don't want to miss anything or anyone you may know.

There is a well-known private club in Los Angeles frequented by the most celebrated stars in Hollywood. For most people, it would be hard to maintain eye contact while talking to someone and resist looking around at Sean Penn, Madonna, Rob Lowe, Farrah Fawcett, Ryan O'Neal, Jack Nicholson, Jane Fonda, and Warren Beatty, who may all walk past within a fifteen-minute period.

However, a person who is an excellent communicator would pay attention to the person he is with and make that person feel as though he or she were the most important person in the world.

George Hamilton, Warren Beatty, and Burt Reynolds are three of the best communicators in Hollywood. Most people who know these men report that when you are with them you feel like the most important person around. I can certainly appreciate what these people are saying about these men after seeing George Hamilton and his date at a restaurant. Even though the entire restaurant was gawking at George, his eyes remained fixed on the lovely lady he was with.

Former Miss America and *PM Magazine* hostess Debra Maffett, who is a former client of mine, also has excellent eye contact. She is not only a gracious hostess but makes you feel extremely important when she talks to you even though there are crowds of people around her trying to get her attention.

I have also found that the successful corporate executives and politicians I have worked with have excellent eye contact. Perhaps that is the reason they became successful—they focus directly on the people they talk to.

Most people don't even realize what a negative and alienating effect their poor eye contact has on their total image. Looking up or down or from side to side when you are thinking is a very bad habit that is all too common. It gives the impression that you are shifty and cannot be trusted.

One of my clients, a cardiologist, had a habit of looking all around the room when he broke bad news to patients regarding their heart conditions. Patients refused to believe him and sought another opinion. This happened so often that the doctor came in to see me to work on developing better eye contact.

Another one of my clients was an attorney who had such poor eye contact that he would look up and to the sides of and over his clients' heads. When he spoke he would find his clients turning their heads in the direction he was looking, to see if something else was going on in the room. The attorney came to see me to help him break his bad habit after several of his clients boldly asked him what he was looking at and to pay attention to them.

After getting help with their eye contact, the cardiologist and the attorney increased their client loads. It took a lot of work to break their bad habit, but they did it.

Eye Contact Exercises

Good eye contact does not mean staring into another person's eyes and not breaking eye contact. This can make people feel as uncomfortable as not looking at them at all. To have good eye contact you need to look in the general vicinity of a person's eyes. Look at her whole face and then at each of the specific parts: hair, eyes, cheek bones, nose, lips, mouth, and chin. Practice looking at the whole face for five seconds. Next look at each part of the face for five seconds. Then practice looking at the whole face for ten seconds, the eyes for ten seconds, and at each part for five seconds.

Finally, alternate between focusing on the whole face and the eyes at regular intervals of ten seconds each.

Practice this technique when you first meet someone and see if your communication improves. In doing so, you'll make him feel as though he is the only person in the room.

—4—
Breathing

Did you ever wonder how Barbra Streisand holds those notes for so long? She has mastered the art of breath control and voice projection. She uses her entire body, especially her abdominal muscles. International singing star Julio Iglesias does this as well. Many professional performers know how to breathe properly while performing but they get into trouble using their everyday speaking voices. They are not alone, as most people do not breathe properly. Improper breathing affects their speech.

The four most common problems people have with their breathing are: (1) taking in too much air and filling up their upper chests, and not using their abdominal muscles when they speak; (2) not using their breath support to help them get rid of stress; (3) taking in too many little breaths, resulting in a weak voice; or (4) they exhale all of their air and proceed to speak on virtually no air at all.

TUMMY BREATHE, DON'T CHEST HEAVE

The foremost error people make when they breathe is using their upper chest instead of their abdominal muscles. The term "diaphragmatic breathing" is a popular misconception. The diaphragm does not breathe. The diaphragm, a thin membrane located under the lungs, separates the lungs from the stomach and the intestines. The abdominal muscles are the most important muscles in breathing.

Dogs, cats, and babies all use abdominal muscles when they breathe. When we sleep and are completely relaxed, we use our abdominal muscles to breathe. During the day, when stressful situations arise, many of us tighten our upper chest and our throat, and tension results. This can be very damaging to our vocal cords because we put additional strain on them.

Tom has the capacity to have a rich resonant voice. Unfortunately, he takes in so much air filling up his lungs that he puts a great deal of pressure on his vocal cords. He also takes in air through his nose, rather than his mouth, when he speaks. This creates a weak, nasal, and throaty sound. When Tom learned to inhale properly, filling only his abdomen and not his upper chest, the result was the rich, booming voice he always wanted to have.

You don't need to take in large amounts of air when you breathe. This will only fill up your lungs and expand your upper chest. You don't need all that air; just take in a little bit of air to fill up your abdominal area. More air does not necessarily mean more power. As with playing a flute or blowing across a Coke bottle, the smaller the air intake the better the tone. The more air you use, the less tone you get. So when you take in air, remember that "less is more."

I remember saying that to a very buxom star who used too much of her upper chest when she breathed. Her reply was priceless. She said, "My, my, my, Doctor Lillian Glass, telling me that less is more. . . . Well, I think that less is less and more is more and I am sure glad I have got more." Despite this star's clever reasoning, I still say less is more, especially when you inhale to speak.

Relaxation Tummy Breathing Technique

What happens when you get anxious or nervous? You keep taking in air with shallow breaths and do not release it as frequently as normal. Carbon dioxide builds up and increases your anxiety. This gives some people severe headaches. The normal

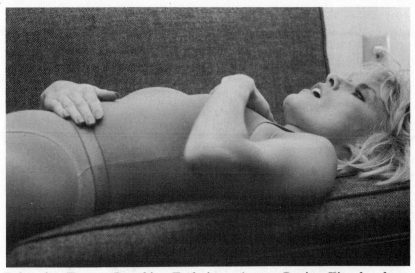

Relaxation Tummy Breathing Technique: Actress Danitza Kingsley demonstrates placing one hand on upper chest and the other on tummy. She breathes in through her mouth for three seconds, holds the breath for three seconds, and then exhales through her mouth for six seconds. *Bill Crite*

breathing cycle takes oxygen in, then lets carbon dioxide out. In order for your body to function normally, this has to happen. Some religions, such as Buddhism and Hinduism, use breath control as a key to inner peace and tranquility. They use breathing to obtain a higher level of consciousness. The long life span of many of the yogis in India and the Himalayas attests to this technique.

The Relaxation Tummy Breathing Technique is a combination of the techniques developed by the ancient yogis in India and a modified version of the technique developed by Dr. Morton Cooper of Los Angeles, California. This technique is the basis for good breath control. It is designed to help calm you down. You can do it in the morning after you wake up and in the evening before you go to sleep. Many of my clients have told me that when they do the exercises in the evening, the technique helps them fall asleep faster. When you do these exercises, do them gently and slowly. Take your time or you

Dolph Lundgren (*Rocky IV* and *Masters of the Universe*) **does the Relaxation Tummy Breathing Technique sitting down. Here he expands his abdomen by taking a breath in through his nose for three seconds, holding it and then contracting his abdominal muscles as he releases the air.** *Firooz Zahedi*

will hyperventilate. Put on a recording of Pachelbel's "Canon in D Minor," or Billy Oskay and Micheal O'Domhnaill's "Nightnoise" (A&M Records) and enjoy. Lie down on your back on a flat surface.

1. (A) Place one hand on your upper chest and one hand on your abdomen. Make sure only your abdomen moves when you are breathing. Don't move your chest. (B) Slowly and gently breathe in through the mouth for three seconds, filling your abdomen with air. (C) Hold for three seconds. (D) Gently and slowly exhale through the mouth for six seconds. You will feel your abdominal muscles contracting as you let all the air out through your mouth. Do this five times.

2. Sitting Up: Next, sit up with head up and shoulders, spine, and back straight. (A) Place one hand on your upper chest and the other on your abdomen. Make sure you keep your upper chest down. (B) Next, gently and slowly breathe in through the mouth for three seconds. Push your abdomen out as you take in the air. (C) Hold the breath for three seconds. (D) Slowly and gently exhale through the mouth for six seconds. Do this five times.

BLOW OUT YOUR TENSION

The Relaxation Tummy Breathing Technique helps calm you down. Another technique will help you release your immediate tension and anger.

Yogi Bikram Choudhury uses breathing techniques to help in muscle relaxation. *Yoga College of India, Beverly Hills*

When someone cuts you off in traffic, do you find yourself tense and holding in all that tension? Do you repress it, or do you release it through expletives and still carry the tension with you throughout the day? By learning the Tension Blow Out Technique, you can oxygenate yourself and let out the anger or negative feelings within you. I have introduced this technique to prisoners in federal and state penitentiaries in California and have reports from the wardens that the technique effectively helps the prison inmates reduce their stress and anxiety and release their anger.

This technique is also good to use when you crack up or burst out laughing at inappropriate times and places. You may not mean to laugh but sometimes you can't help it. This embarrassing situation results from using laughter to release tension.

Dr. Glass shows Ben Vereen the TENSION BLOW-OUT EXERCISES. Ben takes a breath of air in through his mouth, fills up his abdomen, and holds it for three seconds. With all of his strength, he blows out all of the air until his abdominal muscles contract. He then holds his breath for another three seconds and begins the cycle all over again. *Rhonda Spray*

Doing the Tension Blow Out will help you to regain your composure. When you're angry, the technique helps you co-ordinate your breathing with talking (breathe in . . . hold . . . talk, talk, talk on the exhalation). In controlling your anger, holding in the air allows you the split second to decide whether you should let the other person have it or let the anger die out with your breath flow.

Tension Blow-Out Exercise

1. Take a breath in through your mouth for three seconds.
2. Hold it for three seconds.
3. Blow out air until you have no air left. Keep pushing until you are completely out of air.
4. Do not breathe for three seconds.
5. Now breathe in for three seconds and repeat steps 1–4 three times. Afterward, proceed to breathe normally. You may feel a little light-headed; don't worry about it as it will go away. You should feel much better and less angry. If you're still angry, repeat this exercise.

STOP GASPING FOR AIR

Nancy, a thirty-two-year-old school teacher, constantly took in gasping breaths in air. She was very excitable in the classroom and had difficulty projecting her voice. She hardly let out any air when she spoke. As a result, she complained of dizziness.

When she changed her breathing patterns using the Relax-ation Tummy Breathing Technique, she became more relaxed and felt much better about her ability to project her voice and be heard. Her headaches disappeared because she was giving her body more oxygen.

Stanley, one of the most annoying speakers I've ever heard, had a weak and wavery voice and sounded like a wimpy little mouse. He would take in a breath of air after every three words, which was not only damaging to his vocal cords but also dam-aging to the listeners' nerves. He didn't have heart or lung trouble, and therefore had no reason to be so short of breath whenever he spoke. Stanley needed to build up more subglottic pressure (pressure underneath the vocal cords) when he spoke. In essence, he needed to build up enough air pressure. By filling up his abdominal area, holding the air in, and then exhaling, he was able to produce more powerful and less irritating sounds.

Kirk Kilgore, an Olympic champion and world-class professional volleyball player sustained a spinal cord injury while playing volleyball in Italy. The injury left this gorgeous six-foot four-inch muscular athlete paralyzed from the neck down. His breathing was shallow and it was difficult for him to speak. He did not control his airflow and had a tendency to expel his entire breath of air before speaking. The result was that he spoke on no air, which made it difficult for him to be heard. He also took in numerous small breaths every few seconds, which would literally exhaust him when he spoke.

After learning to use the Sustained Football Player Voice Technique, he can sustain his tones longer and has a deeper and richer voice quality. If you did not see Kirk in his wheelchair, you would never know that he was paralyzed. His improved breath control has made his sports commentaries on cable TV's Prime Ticket KNX Radio and ABC Sports much smoother. Kirk has even developed more confidence in his abilities as a public speaker. His great vocal control through the use of this exercise has allowed him to venture into new areas where he has to make maximum use of his voice—as an actor and in doing radio and television commercials.

One of my clients, a handsome, well-known film director and producer in Hollywood, has the best breath support I have ever seen. He can hold a tone on one breath for over sixty seconds, well above the average time of twenty seconds. Unfortunately, this great breath support did not carry over to his speech. He took short little breaths about every five seconds when he spoke, instead of taking in a small breath and talking for as long as he could. By letting all of his air out, he put such a severe strain on his vocal cords that he lost his voice. By using the Sustained Football Player Voice Technique, he was able to maximize his excellent breath control.

Sustained Football Player Voice Technique

The following technique is based on European vocal techniques of the 1940s and 1950s. This technique helps project the voice, oxygenate the blood, eliminate tension, and control the rate of speech.

Using the technique while speaking involves taking a breath of air in and letting your words out with the exhalation. Let air out slowly, and speak on the air stream. Good speech results from breathing properly and releasing a controlled flow of air for speaking.

Five-time NFL all-pro Lester Hayes of the L.A. Raiders demonstrates the Sustained Football Player Voice Technique. He takes a breath in through his mouth for three seconds, holds it, opens his jaw and the back of his throat, and makes a deep hollow sound. *Chrissy Ogden*

While sitting up:

1. (A) gently breathe in through your mouth for three seconds; (B) hold for three seconds; and (C) exhale, dropping your jaw wide and placing your tongue behind your lower teeth, making sure the back portion of your tongue is concave or looking as though it is scooped out. Open the back of the throat as though you were yawning. Pretend a hollow tube runs from the back of your throat all the way down to your tummy.

2. On the exhalation of the "yawn," keep your jaw open, and let out a "hah" sound for as long you can. Remember to open the back of your throat.

3. Feel the tone pass all the way down the imaginary hollow tube from your mouth, resonating down the back of your throat to your stomach.

4. The sound you will make will be low and deep. Imagine a big football player with a deep voice as you make this tone. Feel the tone resonate and vibrate deep in your stomach. Remember to hold the tone for six seconds. Do this exercise slowly and in a relaxed manner, sitting up, so you don't get light-headed. Do it five times.

In doing these exercises, don't feel self-conscious and put your hand in front of your mouth to cover a yawn. Be sure not to stifle your yawn. Instead, use your air to exhale the "ha" sound, opening the back of your throat.

BREATHE AND SLOW DOWN

For the most part it is better to talk too fast than too slow. Studies have shown that people who talk faster are judged to be more intelligent and credible than those who talk slower, but you can talk too fast. The problem is that the listener oftentimes doesn't hear everything you're trying to say and must constantly ask you to repeat what you said. This annoys you as well as the listener. Talking too fast is such an annoying habit that our survey showed that close to 70 percent responded negatively to it.

Most people talk too fast because of faulty breath support.

They don't use their breathing capacity to help sustain their tones. They take in little breaths of air after every few words. They let out all their air before they make a sound. They don't coordinate their breathing with their talking because they are usually out of air before beginning to speak; they talk faster to get everything out on their minimal breath. The typical results are choppy and breathy tones.

Slow-Down Exercises

1. The Sustained Football Player Voice Technique can help you slow down your speech as you learn to take in a breath of air, hold it, and release it for as long as you can. This exercise helps you to better coordinate your breathing with talking on an extended exhalation of air.

2. Practice taking a breath and holding it. Open the back of your throat and begin to talk until you're out of air. Be sure to feel your tummy muscles contracting until you are completely out of air before you take in another breath. Repeat this cycle over and over again as often as possible during the day in your conversations at work and with friends. Eventually it will become a habit and your talking will become a little slower.

—5—
Voice

HOW IMPORTANT IS YOUR TONE OF VOICE?

The tone of a person's voice can be so annoying that it can endanger his or her life. Yes, you read this correctly. You may think that this statement is rather dramatic or even funny. In fact, you may jokingly say to yourself, "Yeah, I've heard such annoying voices that if I had to listen to them all the time, they would drive me insane or to my grave."

Recently, a writer from *The New York Times* who interviewed me wanted to know whether I, as a voice and communications specialist, felt that there was any merit to the many complaints lodged by pilots against the irritating voices they heard from the control tower. My feelings are that these pilots do indeed have something to gripe about and that their complaints should not be overlooked or taken lightly.

We know from research that when we hear an irritating voice over a period of time, two things happen. Either we become agitated and irritable or we tune out. This can affect a pilot's judgement and performance. Perhaps the reason that there have been so many airplane crashes in the past year is the fact that we have allowed air traffic controllers with annoying voices to guide our pilots toward their landings.

When we become agitated, our heart rate, pulse rate, and perspiration level increase and our breathing patterns change.

This affects our physical behavior. Most of us tune annoying people out. We can recall this in our childhood experiences. When mom or dad asked us to do something or badgered us about cleaning our room, many of us tuned them out.

This common occurrence may seem like a harmless thing to do if you are a child, but if you subconsciously tune out an irritating voice or if others "tune you out" because of your voice the results can be devastating.

In this chapter you will learn how to get rid of annoying vocal habits and develop a healthier, more powerful, and sexier voice. You will also find out how to develop more emotion in your voice, which will not only make you more appealing in the business world but will also give you greater sex appeal in your personal life. You will discover how to have fun with your voice through singing and how to use your voice to defend yourself.

Your voice is such a powerful psychological mechanism that it can calm people or make them nervous. You've heard about nervous pet owners having nervous dogs and calm pet owners having calm, obedient dogs. Well, your voice can affect your dog's personality.

Most animal trainers will verify this. Using a loud or hard voice may result in a cowering, fearful, or even aggressive dog. Using a calm, smooth voice may relax the dog. The tone you use can have a positive or negative effect on how the dog relates to you.

This is also the case with children. Research shows that babies are sensitive to voice patterns. If you use harsh attacking sounds in front of most newborns, you'll startle them and they'll start to wail in order to let you know they are angry and annoyed. As adults, we may not wail but we show that we are annoyed in other ways. We back off, contort our facial muscles, or tune out what the other person is saying.

My survey revealed that the habits we are most turned off by relate to the tones of our voices. Eighty percent of the people polled were especially irritated by mumbling, soft voices. Seventy-three percent found monotonous, boring voices and too-loud voices annoying, while 61 percent found a too-high-pitched voice disturbing.

Do Voices Age?

I always get annoyed whenever elderly people are parodied on television and stereotyped as having slow, monotonous voices. Many people think that the elderly sound like they do because of their age and that their vocal cords get weaker as they grow older. There is very little research to substantiate this. I believe that people, no matter what their age, can sound as old as they feel. If you feel old and frail and lifeless, it will be reflected in your voice. On the other hand, if you feel that you have meaning in your life, this too will be demonstrated in your voice. So no matter what your age, you're as young as you sound.

Listen to the voices of celebrities like George Burns, Helen Hayes, Diana Vreeland, and Milton Berle. It certainly is difficult to tell their exact ages because these people use vocal inflection and sound as though they are full of excitement and life.

We know that producer and *American Bandstand* host Dick Clark must be approaching his sixties. He clearly illustrates how difficult it is to tell a person's age from his voice. Many of us remember him as he was in his thirties, and he still sounds as vivacious and exciting as he did then. His voice is so energetic and animated that it's difficult to tell what age he is, both by his looks and by the sound of his voice.

It's not age but abuse that causes most old-sounding voices. Most of us take our voices for granted. The only time most of us pay any attention to them is when we're singing in the car or in the shower and can't hit a note. Otherwise we become conscious of our voice only when we have a problem with it; when we're hoarse, lose our voice, have pain in the throat, or have to see a physician or speech pathologist. Many people abuse their voices without being aware of it until it's too late— after they have developed a vocal problem (hoarseness or voice loss) due to their abuse. They ravage their vocal cords by smoking, drinking heavily, talking over noise, talking too much, constantly taking breaths of air in and letting them out and speaking on virtually no air, attacking their sounds, and talking at a vocal pitch that is either too high or too low for them.

FOURTEEN RULES FOR VOCAL HEALTH

Although I treat many celebrities, business people, and professionals who are in the public eye and use their voices more than the average person, I am convinced that any of us can develop vocal problems if we are not careful. If you want to have a healthy voice, you need to develop good vocal habits and follow these rules so that you don't abuse your voice.

1. No smoking. This is the biggest culprit in vocal devastation. You might think that a smoker's voice is sexy, but if you took a look at the smoker's vocal cords you would change your mind. There's nothing sexy about cancerous cords. You're probably sick of hearing how cigarette smoking causes cancer, but its importance can't be diminished. Having treated several patients who have had to have their vocal cords removed because of cancer, I am a strong advocate of no smoking. Cancer affecting the vocal cords is one of the worst things that can happen to a person because the smoker also dies an emotional death by not being able to speak.

2. No drugs, except by prescription. They are irritants to the vocal mechanism.

3. No alcohol. It causes the vocal cords to swell. If you do drink, limit your alcohol intake.

4. Don't sleep with your mouth open. This can dry out the vocal cords. That's why your voice sounds low in the morning. I know that it's easier said than done, but consciously try to go to sleep with your mouth closed. You should also sleep with a humidifier.

5. Don't yell or scream. Everyone overdoes it sometimes: mothers who shout at their children, clergymen who give long sermons, entertainers who have to sing or talk non-stop for hours in smoke-filled rooms, attorneys in the courtroom, teachers, and children yelling on the playground. However, if you don't want to abuse your voice, you can't yell, scream or shout. It's murdering your vocal cords.

6. Don't talk over noise. Talking over noise is a major factor in vocal abuse. Simply sit very close to the person you are conversing with. Use breath spray if you're self-conscious and don't

shout. If you have to be heard, use a megaphone or bullhorn as needed. If a bullhorn is too conspicuous for you, try an electronic microphone. The cordless variety gives you more mobility. Many aerobics instructors find them helpful in cutting down on their vocal abuse.

7. Don't clear your throat. Chronic throat clearing is another problem. If you have to clear your throat, use your abdominal muscles to push up the phlegm and not your vocal cords. You may also want to check with a physician to give you some medication to dry up your postnasal drip.

8. Don't talk too much or too loudly. Incessant talking and talking too loudly can also contribute to vocal abuse. So limit your conversations and extraneous talking. Speak only when you have to. This also helps keep you from sticking your foot in your mouth so often.

9. Keep your throat lubricated. Carry glycerine-based throat lozenges and use them whenever you need to.

10. Limit consumption of milk products. They create mucus which causes you to clear your throat more.

11. Drink plenty of water. Ten to twelve glasses of water a day will help keep your throat moist and help you to lose weight as well.

12. Use steam twice a day, morning and evening. Get a facial steamer or just turn on the hot water in the shower or sink and breathe it in for three to five minutes. You'll be surprised at how it opens you up.

13. Open the back of your throat when you speak to take pressure off your vocal cords.

14. Use your tummy muscles. Bear down and out on your tummy muscles to produce richer tones and to stop vocal abuse.

Rules 13 (Opening your throat) and 14 (Using your tummy muscles) are two of the most important rules for developing good vocal habits.

OPEN YOUR THROAT

Most people develop problems with their voices because they put too much tension on their vocal cords—a muscle the size of a thumbnail. They close off the backs of their throats and the vocal tract, which is the hollow tube from the lips to the abdominal muscles, when they speak. The air doesn't pass through this tract, so the vocal cords rub together and become irritated. If the cords are irritated for a long period of time, they may develop growths, nodules or polyps. The resulting sound is hoarse and breathy. Often, the person will lose his voice.

You can tell if someone is closing off the back of his throat if you hear an unpleasant crackling sound when he speaks. This is called a "glottal fry." It is irritating to both the speaker and the listener.

There are three things you can do to help you open the back of your throat and eliminate this "glottal fry."

The Ka-Ga-Ha Exercise

This exercise is designed to help you release the muscular tension from your vocal cords and help you open you vocal tract so that you make rich, full, resonating tones.

It trains you to use the muscles in the back of your throat so that you can control and open up the back of your throat when you speak.

1. Take a breath in through the mouth and open the back of your throat as you did in Sustained Tone Exercise. As you exhale, say "Ka, ka, ka, ka, ka" in one breath. Do this five times.

2. Repeat the first step, saying "Ga, ga, ga, ga, ga."

3. Repeat the first step, alternating "Ka, ga, ka, ga, ka, ga."

4. Repeat the first step, alternating "Ka, ga, ha, ka, ga, ha."

Remember to use only one breath each time!

SPEAK UP: HOW TO PROJECT

Besides opening the back of your throat, you need to use your tummy muscles to anchor the tones in your vocal tract. When you talk, you need to put pressure on your bigger and stronger stomach muscles and not on your smaller and weaker throat

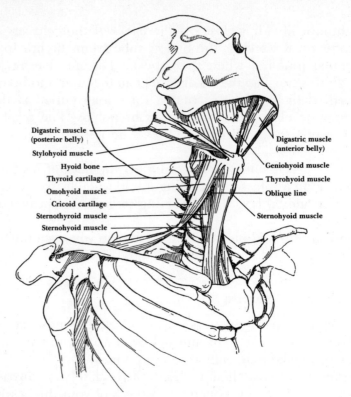

Digastric muscle
(posterior belly)

Stylohyoid muscle

Hyoid bone

Thyroid cartilage

Omohyoid muscle

Cricoid cartilage

Sternothyroid muscle

Sternohyoid muscle

Digastric muscle
(anterior belly)

Geniohyoid muscle

Thyrohyoid muscle

Oblique line

Sternohyoid muscle

Extrinsic Laryngeal Muscles

muscles. Doing this keeps you from hurting your vocal cords
and helps you control your voice so that it doesn't crack.

In both opening the back of your throat and pushing or
bearing down and out on your tummy muscles when you speak,
you will produce a richer, more powerful, and deeper voice.
Nobody will ever have to ask you to speak up again. The Gallup
poll shows that 80 percent of the people questioned felt that
not projecting your voice or mumbling is one of the most annoying habits you can have. It was one of the top three most
annoying talking habits.

It is frustrating to listen to a person who mumbles and who
doesn't speak up, like the Mumbling Millionaire or Ralph, the
Rodney Dangerfield-like character we discussed in chapter 2,
who didn't get any respect.

Even though I love Marlon Brando's acting talents, I find it frustrating to watch him because he mumbles so much that I can't hear half of what he's saying. Even though Marlon Brando's mumbling hasn't hurt his appeal at the box office, just think how much greater his appeal would be if you could understand him better.

By using your tummy muscles to project your voice, you can stop mumbling and even become more powerful in your interactions with other people. This happened to Robert Lamm, lead singer for the group Chicago, who tells about the difference in his life since he learned to project his voice. He says:

> My voice comes across with more power and more conviction. I'm more sure of what I say and what I'm talking about.
>
> I get the most practice when the phone rings because, for some reason, when the phone rings, the act of going over to answer it and picking it up off of the receiver sets up that whole mechanism where you take in a breath, hold it, push out your stomach muscles, and then speak into the phone. So the most comments that I get about my voice are from people on the other end of the phone.
>
> If they know me and they know that I am seeing, they say, "Oh, I love your new voice." But otherwise, it seems as if the conversation has more focus, or at least I'm more focused.
>
> For example, I had an idea and I wanted to call everybody else in the band to set up a rehearsal schedule. Now this is something that I sort of dread doing because in the context of the band, if one person has an idea, it takes forever politically to get everyone else aligned to accomplish something.
>
> So generally when you have and idea it is best to have two or three guys already in agreement with you to convince the other three or four guys.
>
> What I did recently was just start with one guy, communicate my idea, say why I thought it was a great idea. But I did it with a voice like I really knew what I was talking about and really knew what I wanted to do.
>
> The first guy said it was a great idea, let's do it. I just called everybody up and by the end of the afternoon, everybody was in agreement with me. Everybody was excited about the idea that I conveyed and what I wanted to accomplish.

I even got some good feedback and incorporated some of that feedback. So what I am saying is that the conviction in the voice in which I presented the idea and the proposal manifested itself. And it actually became a reality.

HELP FOR PROBLEM VOICES

Exercises for Too-Soft Voices

The following exercises are designed to help you develop your tummy muscles, project your voice, and speak in flowing tones from your tummy muscles. The exercises will also keep you from mumbling and dying off at the end of sentences. They will enable you to generate your tones from your tummy and not your throat. Pushing down and out on your tummy muscles properly will help you physically push the air out through your lungs, your esophagus, the back of your throat and your lips.

In doing these exercises, remember to keep the back of your throat open so you don't close off your tones.

Lester Hayes demonstrates the Heel-Toe Bounces, which allow gravity to help bounce out tones. *Chrissy Ogden*

Bob Beck demonstrates chair pulls (left) and chair pushes (right) to help strengthen his abdominal muscles for speaking. *Bill Crite*

1. Heel-Toe Bounces: Stand on your toes and then drop to your heels as you maintain an "Ah" sound. Do this ten times. You will feel the tones being pushed down and vibrating in your abdominal area. You can also do this with a trampoline. The technique of using a portable trampoline was devised by Professor J. Kephart in the 1940s, who used the technique to work with children with cerebral palsy. As the children were bounced on the trampoline, they made sounds which were projected by gravity helping to push out their tones. I found a similar technique used with non-handicapped people to be extremely effective. As you bounce on the trampoline and say "Ah," holding it for as long as you can, you'll find that your tone is richer and louder when it is generated from your tummy muscles.

2. Chair Pulls: This technique is based on a modified version of Dr. Daniel R. Boone's technique to help project the voice. Sit in a chair and pull up on it and release it five times in succession as you maintain the "Ah" sound for as long as you can. You will feel the tones vibrating in your tummy. Do this five times. You can also do this exercise in your car, gently pulling up on your steering wheel as you drive.

3. Chair Pushes: This technique is also based on a modified version of Dr. Boone's technique. Push down instead of pulling up on the chair, pushing and releasing it five times in succession. Once again you should feel the tones vibrating in your tummy. Do this exercise five times. You can also do it in your car by gently pushing down on your steering wheel when you are stopped.

4. Hand Clasps: Clasp your finger tips together with your elbows stretched out. Try to pull your arms apart and then release as you say "Ah." You should feel your abdominal muscles working as you try to pull your arms apart. Do this exercise five times in succession, sustaining the "Ah" sound without dying off at the end. Many opera singers use this technique to gain more abdominal support to help them reach certain notes.

5. Tummy Bounce Ha-Ha's: This exercise not only helps you develop control over your tummy muscles, but releases the pressure from your throat muscles as well. Take a breath in through

Gloria Loring clasps her finger tips together with elbows stretched out. She says "ah" and feels her abdominal muscles working to help project her voice. *Bill Crite*

Matt Lattanzi demonstrates the Tummy Bounce Ha-Ha's as he opens up the back of his throat and pushes his abdominal muscles down and out ten times in succession, using one breath. *Bill Crite*

the mouth for three seconds and immediately let it out as you say ten "Ha"s in succession, using one breath. You should feel your tummy bouncing as you push down and out on your tummy muscles.

If you aren't able to do all ten "Ha"s in succession on one breath, you are: (a) letting too much air out at once, or (b) you're not opening the back of the throat, or (c) you're not bouncing your tummy muscles and pushing them down and out. You need to do all of these things together in order to do the exercise properly. If you're not, keep working on it. You will get it eventually.

6. Tummy Flows: Take a breath in through the mouth and open the back of your throat. Say the letters ABCD, flowing each letter into the next as though it were one word. Do not break the air flow. Push your tummy muscles down and out as you flow out the sounds. In all of the exercises, take a breath

in for three seconds, opening the back of the throat and flowing out the block of four sounds, pushing your tummy down and out.

AY-BEE-CEE-DEE	(ABCD)
EE-YEF-JEE-YACH	(EFGH)
I-JAY-KAY-YELL	(IJKL)
EM-MEN-NO-PEE	(MNOP)
KEYOU-WAR-RES-TEE	(QRST)
YOU-VEE-DOUBLE YOU-WEX	(UVWX)
WY-ZEE-YA-BEE	(YZAB)

Quiet Down a Too-Loud Voice

Do people complain that you speak too loudly? If they do, you had better listen to them and do something about it because it is one of the five most annoying talking habits.

Close to 75 percent of the people tested in our Gallup poll were disturbed by voices that were too loud.

Speaking too loudly can also damage your vocal cords. You can probably understand this better if you have ever observed people who talk too loudly. Usually, you'll notice the veins and muscles in their necks popping out when they speak. They usually close off their throat muscles and try to squeeze out their sounds instead of using their abdominal muscles to help them project their tones. The results are severe vocal irritation and damage due to the stress and strain they put on their vocal cords.

Why do people speak so loudly? Well, many people speak too loudly because they have a hearing loss. If this is the case, get a hearing check-up and if you need a hearing aid, get one. Don't be self-conscious about it. Nowadays, there are micro-hearing aids which can be worn inside the ear. They are in-conspicuous and have the capacity to amplify your hearing so that you don't need to talk so loudly. For most people, a hearing problem isn't the cause. Most people talk loudly because they are used to yelling over noise or shouting in front of large groups of people, the way aerobic instructors do.

Most aerobic instructors trade off having a terrific body for having a terrible voice. All of their shouting and yelling not only creates vocal problems, but they often carry an unpleasant speaking voice out of the gym.

It is important to control your loudness because it's unpleasant to hear someone talking loudly as if unaware of their environment.

A television personality I worked with who was concerned about her privacy off the set, once told me that everyone seemed to recognize her by her voice. Even though she dressed down at the drug store or supermarket or at a restaurant and wasn't her usual glamorous, made-up self, she said that everyone seemed to look at her whenever she spoke. She thought that they recognized her just by the sound of her voice.

By asking her if it wasn't the volume of her voice that caused people to recognize her, I brought her loudness problem to her attention. I told her that she practically shouted when she was in public. Prior to this she was unaware of her bad habit. When she learned to become more mindful, she won back her anonymity in public places.

Another example of how negatively people can react to an overly loud voice can be seen in a case I observed while vacationing in Hawaii.

A group of people was sprawled out sunning in the sand. A man in this group had been lulled to sleep by the rhythmic gentle swishing sounds of the waves. While he was asleep, two women plopped themselves directly in front of him. All of a sudden this man's body shot straight up as he was awakened by the horrible cackling screams, yelling, and loud talking of one of the women. She had total disregard for everyone around her. She was oblivious to the fact that other people around her perhaps wanted a little peace and quiet and had come to Hawaii to get away from people like her. The man tried to ignore the annoying bursts of loudness but his already frayed nerves got the best of him. He burst out yelling, "Listen, you hyena, shut your damn mouth!" Everyone around him applauded and the two ladies left.

I certainly wouldn't recommend that you use this man's exact words, but I do give him a lot of credit for mirroring the woman's behavior. She wasn't aware of just how offensive she was until someone pointed it out to her in a way that reflected her own obnoxiously loud voice. Maybe she learned from this experience, maybe she didn't. But in any event, I learned a great deal from observing the entire scene. I learned how little patience we have with people who talk so loudly that they upset the air waves around us and hurt our eardrums. However, most people's reactions aren't as forceful as this man's. Most people just walk away and never give people like this lady a second chance, especially if it's in a business or personal situation.

If you are a loud talker:

1. Get your hearing checked. See a qualified audiologist as well as an otolaryngologist to get a thorough examination.

2. If you don't have a hearing loss you might want to use your family and friends for feedback. Ask them to tell you when you are talking too loudly, but make sure you tell them to be gentle about reminding you.

3. Be mindful at all times in every situation until it becomes a habit for you to speak at an appropriate level. Pay attention to people around you. Often there are nonverbal cues given to those who speak inappropriately loud, such as pulling away, facial grimaces, and no eye contact.

4. To have better control over your loudness, get a tape recorder with a volume meter on it and practice reading and speaking into the recorder. Try to keep the volume of your voice at such a level that the pointer on the meter doesn't deviate to the right (the red area on some meters). Try to keep the pointer on the midline as you speak. This will help you regulate your volume. Focus your attention on the meter. Do this exercise for ten minutes twice a day and you'll be surprised at how much control you'll have over your loudness.

OPTIMUM PITCH LEVEL (OPL)

At what pitch should you be speaking? In order to avoid speaking too high or too low, you need to find your Optimum Pitch Level, or OPL. It is important to find the OPL of your voice and speak a little above or a little below that level.

The OPL should feel comfortable to you and is the pitch you need to use every time you speak. Otherwise you may damage your vocal cords.

In the diagram below the straight horizontal line represents the OPL. The sound wave is the squiggly line above and below it. Ideally, you should be speaking at the horizontal line and approximately two notes above it and two notes below it.

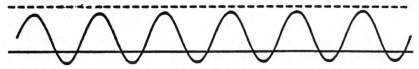

People who speak at too high a pitch tend to speak at the point where the top dotted line is. Speaking like this on a regular basis can hurt your vocal cords. Singer Michael Jackson is guilty of speaking like this.

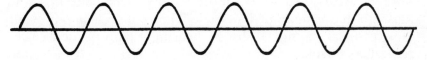

Conversely, those who speak on the bottom dotted line too much below their OPL can also hurt their vocal cords. Henry Kissinger is guilty of doing this and producing a glottal fry.

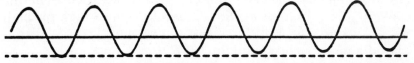

In order to have a healthy voice, you need to use all of your pitch range (two notes above and two notes below your OPL) periodically throughout your speech. Doing this adds more excitement and meaning to what you're trying to say.

Find Your OPL

Take a small breath in, filling up your tummy. Remember to keep your upper chest down. As you exhale say "Ah ha" as though you were agreeing with someone. (This is similar to the technique described by Dr. Morton Cooper of Los Angeles in the literature who uses "Um hum" instead of "Ah ha.") Next, tummy-punch out the tone, pushing under your breastbone so that a wavering tone comes out. This sound is your OPL. Make sure the tone feels comfortable.

Too-High Pitch

I asked people if they were more annoyed by a voice that was too high in a woman or in a man. The results came out even. Most of us are annoyed just by hearing a high-pitched voice, regardless of sex.

Some men, like singer Michael Jackson, speak in a high-pitched voice on purpose, thinking that they are protecting their voices from vocal strain. What they don't realize is that by using the upper end of their vocal cords they are straining their voices even more. People who constantly do this may get into a great deal of trouble down the road and develop nodules on their vocal cords because the vocal cords are constantly hitting together in an unnatural position.

Although a high-pitched voice is annoying to over 60 percent of us as determined by the survey, most of us find a high-pitched voice rather humorous, especially if the voice is used intentionally for a comedy role like Jennifer Tilly's rocket scientist in the comedy *Moving Violations*. Randi Brooks used a high-pitched nasal voice in *The Man With Two Brains,* and Treat Williams played a high-pitched hunk in *The Ritz.*

Unfortunately, we also laugh at people with high-pitched voices and find it hard to take them seriously even when they don't intend to be funny, as in the case of Dr. Ruth Westheimer. Many people have told me that they listen to this sex therapist only because they find her high-pitched voice and exaggerated German accent hysterical, even though in most cases Dr. Ruth doesn't intend to be funny.

Silent movie star John Gilbert was literally laughed off the screen never to perform again when the audiences who swooned and fantasized about this silent sex symbol heard his thin, high-pitched voice in the talkies. Had he used the techniques in this book to lower his voice, he might have been around a lot longer.

Mr. Gilbert's problem was probably that he didn't make the vocal transition from adolescence to manhood.

I have worked with several young actors in their twenties and thirties who have had this problem. It's a very common problem. When a male goes through puberty, one of the first things he experiences is that his voice cracks. An adolescent boy isn't very comfortable with this because it embarrasses him. His classmates or a brother or sister may laugh at him or a parent may innocently bring the matter to his attention, causing further embarrassment. In his attempts to control this cracking he may tighten up his vocal cords, which will lead to a higher-pitched voice. Often, the adolescent boy will carry this habit into adulthood and the result is an inappropriately high-pitched voice.

I've worked with hundreds of men who have had this problem. These men have been from all walks of life: stockbrokers, CPA's, attorneys, professors, salesmen, actors. It's a very common problem and it's very simple to correct.

I used the techniques in this section to help lower the voices of several celebrities, like Matt Lattanzi (*My Tutor*), Dolph Lundgren, and Rob Lowe, who was able to have a deeper, richer, and sexier voice which helped him in his performance in *About Last Night*. The critics who raved about his acting in the movie consistently made references to Rob's "sexy voice."

Rob Lowe has great things to say about the technique. When I asked him how he felt this program changed the sound of his voice, his reply was:

> I feel that my voice is stronger and doesn't break up as it used to.
> I got a great compliment from my sound man the other day on my voice. He said I had a beautiful voice that was easy to mix and modulate. No one has ever said anything like that to me before.
> I told him, "I've got to go call Dr. Glass. She's going to love this!"

By learning to lower the pitch of their voices and sounding more masculine, many of the young male hunks I have worked with have gone on to do meatier roles instead of the beefcake roles they did in the past.

Talking with a high-pitched voice doesn't only affect men. Women are also guilty of hanging on to the little-girl or cartoon-like Betty Boop or baby voices they used when they were younger. Often, these Betty Boop-type voices sound cute at ages ten and twelve but sound bad at age twenty and even worse at age forty. Talking like a little girl often reinforces feelings of helplessness, insecurity, and a lack of self-confidence.

Actress Melanie Griffith (*Body Double* and *Something Wild*) had the following things to say about her former high-pitched voice and about how the program has affected her life:

"Before working with you, my voice was always a drawback to me personally and to my work. Who wants to hire a 28 year old who speaks like she's thirteen? No one! You've changed my life. And you have given me the confidence to believe in myself. . . . You have helped me to get in touch with myself."

Melanie's feelings are like those of so many others. As a woman, it's important to modify the pitch of your voice, especially if you're in business. Most people tend to doubt a woman's credibility as well as her general capabilities if she talks in too high a pitch. Individuals may not take her seriously or may even tune her out, as the following example shows.

A few years ago I attended a conference on birth defects where a panel of three men and three women spoke on the topic of genetic abnormalities. For the most part, the audience was attentive and eagerly listening to the speakers. However, I observed that whenever two of the women, who had high-pitched baby voices, spoke, there was more inattentiveness by the audience. I noticed that people in the audience were restless as they whispered to people next to them and shuffled their feet more than when the three men and the lower-voiced woman spoke.

Many women have been made painfully aware of the effect that their high-pitched voices has on their chances for promotion. Often, women come to see me because they have received negative evaluations from their companies about the sound of their voices. In almost all cases their voices are too high. By helping them to consistently lower their voices, I help them to develop more self-confidence, which makes them even more productive.

Studies have shown that the pitch of your voice can be a determining factor in whether or not you're telling the truth about something. In fact, Professor Paul Ekman of the University of California at San Francisco found that the pitch of people's voices becomes higher when they lie. Research has also shown that those with higher pitched voices are perceived as being less credible than those with lower pitched voices.

I remember a male professor I once had who had a high-pitched voice. Students constantly seemed to doubt his credibility, openly questioning the validity of his statements throughout his lectures. Somehow, we never fully believed what he was telling us because he sounded like a little kid who was lying to us.

So, if you want people to believe you and have more faith in you, you need to lower the pitch of your voice.

What to Do to Lower Your Pitch

1. First find your OPL by using the Dr. Morton Cooper technique.

2. Holding the OPL (Ha), glide down two notes from it. These lower notes should feel comfortable. You should not strain to make these notes. They should come naturally. Remember to open up the back of your throat and push your tummy down and out as you make these two lower notes.

3. Repeat step 2, only this time say these sentences. (Make sure you glide your pitch down to the two notes below your OPL, especially at the end of the sentences.):

(a) Come
      see
         me.

(b) I
   will
      go.

(c) I
   love
      you.

Repeat these sentences five times.

In most cases a low-pitched voice is considered an asset. Studies have shown that men and women who have lower voices are perceived as being sexually exciting, sensuous, and credible. In fact, Dr. Paul Ekman's research found that people who spoke with lower-pitched voices were perceived as lying less. His research was further validated when he found that when people lied, their pitch level got higher. Dr. Ekman also found that people with lower voices were judged to be more sociable and more relaxed.

Our own experience verifies Dr. Ekman's study. Listen to the newscasters on all three networks (Peter Jennings, Dan Rather, and Tom Brokaw). They wouldn't be there if they didn't have low-pitch and credible sounding voices. For a man to sound credible and strong, his voice needs to be lower-pitched.

In the past, low voices in women were considered unique and an oddity. Women like Tallulah Bankhead, Marlene Dietrich, Gloria Swanson, and Lauren Bacall were perceived as being strong, powerful, and sensuous.

Today, these perceptions still hold true. For a woman to be successful in business, she needs to use a lower-pitched voice which will make her sound strong and powerful, yet still feminine and sensuous. Elizabeth Taylor's voice, which is low and sensuous, exemplifies this. Our Gallup poll showed that her voice was the highest-rated of all the women in the survey.

Furthermore, we consistently like a man's voice that is lower as shown by the results of the Gallup poll. Actor Bill Cosby, and newsman Dan Rather received the highest rating for their voices. These voices are low-pitched. So your voice is better received if it is lower in pitch. However, it is possible to sound too low.

Many men in their attempts to sound more masculine speak at a pitch that is so low that it can damage their vocal cords. Frequently these men speak so low that they develop a glottal fry (recall the example of Henry Kissinger). If this glottal fry is made on a consistent basis, it might damage the vocal cords. Ulcers can develop on the lower portion of the vocal cords because of the way they hit together. Usually there is pain accompanying these vocal ulcers which radiates to the ear. It often hurts when the person swallows.

I've had several clients who developed these ulcers by speaking at an abnormally low pitch. By showing them how to raise the pitch of their voices just a little and still keep their rich deep voices, the ulcers disappeared. After raising their vocal pitch, they noticed that they didn't have to clear their throats as much and felt none of the vocal strains they had felt in the past. Speaking took less effort. Their voices didn't tire out and die off and their throats didn't hurt anymore.

What to Do to Heighten Your Pitch

1. Find your OPL by using Dr. Cooper's technique.
2. Glide up two notes from the OPL. These higher notes should feel comfortable. You should not strain to get these notes. They should come naturally. Remember to open up the back of your throat and push your tummy down and out as you make these two high notes.
3. Hold the second high-pitched note as long as you can until your tummy muscles contract. Do this ten times.
4. Say each of the following sentences as you make sure you comfortably raise your pitch two notes above your OPL. Be sure to use the second high-pitched note at the end of the sentence.

                            me.
                   see
(A) Come

                   go.
            will
(B) I

                   you.
            love
(C) I

KILLER MONOTONES

A monotonous, boring voice is the number-one killer of interpersonal relationships, especially those between men and women. So much of the meaning of what you really want to say is lost when you lack vocal excitement.

You can tell your wife that she looks beautiful or that she smells nice but if you don't say it in an enthusiastic tone, you're better off keeping your mouth shut.

We are confused by people who speak in a boring monotone; this frustrates us. We doubt their credibility and we find that they get on our nerves more than others we know. We may be more defensive and even more short-tempered with them.

The Gallup survey results confirm these observations. A boring monotonous voice was one of the top four annoying talking habits. Close to 75 percent of the people surveyed were annoyed by a monotonous voice. Now you know why Howard Cosell used to annoy you whenever you watched him on Monday Night Football.

Of all the celebrities in the Gallup survey, Sylvester Stallone received the lowest rating. Close to 50 percent of the people surveyed didn't like the way he sounded. If you examine his voice closely, you will find that his monotone is his biggest verbal turn off. If he learned to use some of the exercises in this section, his voice would become as exciting as his body is.

People who sound monotone are often unsure of themselves. They may not feel comfortable enough with themselves to "let it go" or to "let it out" and express what they feel.

There is a gorgeous young actress whose biggest problem with Hollywood critics is her voice. Critics say she sounds dull, boring, and lifeless. This actress, who literally developed physically in front of the camera, may not have developed emotionally. This is reflected in her empty expression. Because she spent so much time in the public eye, her emotions may have been suppressed. She may have been reprimanded every time she wore her emotions on her sleeve, so to speak. This ultimately stifled her emotional expression and may have resulted in her monotonous voice. With more experience under her belt and with more self-esteem, this actress may be able to express better what's in her heart and counteract the damage.

She is not alone. Many parents squelch their children's emotional expression without even realizing it. As children, we freely spill out our emotions. We squeal when we're happy, we whine when we're hungry, and we wail when we're upset. Too often, we are reprimanded when we freely express ourselves because our parents determine that our timing was inopportune. To avoid the hassles and negative consequences, we often think that it's better just to be quiet and forget about what we are feeling. The result may be that we begin to express ourselves in a boring monotone.

In practicing the exercises in this chapter, we can learn how to put more excitement in our voices and get more in touch with our emotions.

WHAT MAKES A GREAT SPEAKER?

Motivational speakers Leo Buscaglia and Zig Ziglar have made millions of dollars. Why do people spend so much money to hear them? It's because their enthusiasm and excitement make you excited. You feel what they are saying. You feel that you've shared their experiences. You laugh at their happy stories. You choke up at their sad ones. You feel their joy when their tones go up and their sadness when their tones go down. These men aren't afraid to be emotional. They aren't afraid to express their feelings publicly—to raise and lower their pitch, to boom out one word and whisper another, to create a symphony of life through their voices. These men can take a bland, boring, or depressing topic and make it exciting.

You too can sound as exciting as these speakers. The Up-Down Glide Technique will help you exercise your vocal muscles. The Emotion Exercise can help you free up your vocal tones, so that you can let your true feelings out.

Up-Down Glide Technique

1. Say the vowel "ah" and slide up a scale for two notes above your OPL, holding each note for three seconds.

        ah
    ah
Ah (OPL)

Don't strain your voice. Make sure it sounds comfortable to you as you slide up the scale.

2. Slide the "ah" vowel down the scale for two notes below your OPL for three seconds.

Ah (OPL)
   ah
      ah

Once again, this should feel comfortable to you as you go down the scale. Don't strain.

3. Glide up the scale singing "ah" and glide back down the scale again singing "ah" in one breath.

     ah
  ah   ah
ah   ah

Emotion Exercise

Make an "ah" sound as you express the following emotions, paying careful attention to making upward or downward glides. Refer to the photos of Jeffrey Kramer in Chapter 3 on pages 64–66 in order to help you feel the emotions when you produce the "ah" sounds.

1. Sadness
2. Surprise
3. Anger
4. Happiness
5. Fear
6. Disgust
7. Sympathy
8. Love
9. Doubt
10. Boredom

If they all sounded alike, you need to take some time and get in touch with your inner feelings. The following exercise will help you to accomplish this. At the end of the last word in the statement, follow the direction by gliding the pitch up or down as indicated.

You will find that raising or lowering the pitch at the appropriate place makes the statement more emotionally meaningful.

                /cited.
           /o ex/
1. I'm s/

2. I dou\
       \bt it.

          /mazed.
3. I'm a/

4. I'm s\
      \o wor\
         \ried.

5. I ha\
     \te \
       \it.

           /it.
       /ve/
6. I lo/

7. I'm sor\
      \ry.

ANYONE CAN SING

Believe it or not, everyone has a singing voice. You may think you're tone deaf and can't hold a note, but you can sing. Everyone can sing. Seth Riggs, who is a good friend of mine and singing coach to stars like Michael Jackson, Stevie Wonder, and

Bette Midler, has helped good singers sing better and taken people who felt that they couldn't sing and made singers out of them.

Seth uses his own technique, but he also gives people confidence. He helps them get over the belief that they can't carry a note.

Like Seth, I too believe that anyone can sing! I've seen it in my office. People who swore they couldn't carry a tune start sounding like canaries after they discover that they can control their vocal cords using the Up-Down Glide Technique.

Many singers seek professional help from me, not with their singing voices, but with their speaking voices. Often, they have terrific singing voices and use all of the right techniques when they sing. But when they speak, it is a different story. They are ruining their voices, which may in turn affect their performance.

Many of these singers had to cancel concert tours because of constant abuse of their speaking. If singers and speakers would only learn the fourteen vocal rules discussed in this chapter and follow all of the exercises in this book, they would hardly ever experience vocal troubles.

Actress and singer Gloria Loring, who had the top hit song "Friends and Lovers," used the techniques to reduce her vocal problems and has never had difficulties with her voice since doing the program. She says:

> I saw Dr. Glass because I had nodes on my vocal cords. My voice is vitally important to me on many levels. It is my profession, as well as a source of creative fulfillment. I was scared I would never be able to sing well again.
>
> In the first few minutes, she assessed my problem and comforted me by explaining what had happened and exactly how we would proceed to get my voice back to normal.
>
> She helped me understand how emotions, self-image, and stress can affect one's voice and how our vocal presentation affects the way people respond to us.
>
> Dr. Glass's expertise made an enormous difference in my life. She can do the same for you.

Another celebrity who has never had vocal problems since doing the program is the lovely, popular television hostess, Sara Purcell (*Real People*), who a few years ago ruptured a vocal cord while coughing, and was speechless for two weeks. She says:

> For me, being speechless was an intolerable situation. I went to Dr. Glass to help me recover and to learn how to never have this happen again.
>
> What a joy my visits with Dr. Glass became! I learned to use my voice properly and never knew hoarseness like that again.
>
> Now if only she could teach me to carry a tune, I'd be the saloon singer I've always dreamed of. But if she can help me talk as much as I love to without frogs, she can help you too. Read on!

Even yogis have been helped by these techniques to further "enlighten" their voices.

Yogi Bikram Choudhury, President of Yoga College of India, tells of his experiences:

> I have taught big yoga classes every day for the last twenty-five years, averaging sixteen hours a day. I speak constantly. This has hurt my throat and my voice for the last twenty years.
>
> A yogi is not supposed to get these problems, but very few yoga teachers speak as much as I do and teach as many classes as I do.
>
> So I ended up with a big tumor on my vocal cords and I couldn't talk or eat for several weeks. I went to over fifty famous doctors around the globe and nobody could help me. They only told me to stop talking and stop teaching yoga. That was definitely not the solution because yoga is my profession and my life. I need to speak.
>
> Finally, a great doctor in Beverly Hills, Dr. Edward Kantor, suggested that I see Dr. Lillian Glass for speech and voice therapy before he scheduled an operation to remove the colossal tumor, just so I would learn how to use my voice properly.
>
> Dr. Glass's program was so successful that the tumor got smaller and smaller and I didn't require surgery. I learned how to take the pressure off of my vocal cords and incorporate my abdominal muscles during breathing.

It is so similar to the yoga techniques that I teach, only it involves speaking. In my practice of yoga, we learn to what extent you can control your body and mind. I could see the relationship between Dr. Glass's teaching and yoga as it involves controlling your speech by controlling certain muscles.

In a matter of months my whole life changed. My students (many of whom are well-known performers and athletes like Shirley MacLaine, Kareem Abdul-Jabbar, Quincy Jones, Olivia Newton-John, and John McEnroe, who are sensitive to and greatly aware of the voice) were amazed at the progress I made.

I now speak with richer, fuller, more resonant tones that are low, slow, and flowing. I feel great!

How simple the techniques are and how much sense they make! I believe in Dr. Glass's program because it has helped me more than I could ever explain and more than I could ever imagine.

Many top singers I have worked with, such as Gloria Loring, Rita Coolidge, Ben Vereen, and Robert Lamm and many other rock stars, have told me that the vocal exercises in this chapter have helped them with their singing voices. This is because the vocal muscles they are now strengthening are used for singing as well as for speaking.

Most people's voices crack and they can't hit certain notes when they sing because they haven't developed their vocal muscles. What they really need is practice using their vocal cords. In order to get this practice and to work out their vocal muscles, I encourage people to turn on the radio or put their favorite tape into the cassette player and sing along for five minutes a day. You can do this whenever you're driving the car. You'll be surprised at how well you start to carry a tune after one month of doing this. It has worked for many of my clients and I'm sure that it will work for you, too.

You may discover that you're a pretty good singer after all. Singing any of the current popular songs on the radio will help you to exercise your entire vocal range.

Remember to open your jaws and the back of your throat, and use your abdominal muscles by pushing down and out on them whenever you sing or speak. Just let it go, let it loose, and have fun!

USING TONES TO WIN

Just as important as it is to talk your way into things to get you to the top, it's equally important to know how to talk your way out of things.

We've all heard about the pretty girl who talked her way out of a traffic ticket or the high school student who talked his way out of an F or the boyfriend who talked his girlfriend out of ending their relationship. Your initial reaction might be to put these people down. "How dare they be so manipulative!" you might think in disgust.

But is it unfair for these individuals to talk their way out of their particular troubles? You have to admit that they did manage to survive and solve their problems through communication.

I certainly don't advocate a lack of integrity—using cheating and manipulation to solve problems, but I do advocate open, sincere communication.

The pretty girl who talked the police officer out of a ticket was through her communication skills convincing enough that the officer believed her story that it was her first offense and that she didn't realize she was over the speed limit. Whether it was true or not, her talking skills were good enough for the officer to let her go.

The high school student who talked his way out of an F and into an "Incomplete" also must have had talking skills convincing enough to do this. His story that the F would ruin his chances of getting into his Dad's alma mater and keep him off the football team, which would further damage his already strained relationship with his Dad, was effective enough to make his teacher give in.

In the case of the boyfriend, he told his girlfriend that the other girl she saw him with was only an old friend from college who was already engaged and needed some advice about buying a house. He repeatedly assured his girlfriend that he wasn't cheating on her and that he loved only her. He reminded her of all the good times they had had together and expressed his disappointment that she could even think that he would be disloyal to her. His communication skills were so effective that the girlfriend took him back with open arms and apologized for doubting him in the first place.

It wasn't only *what* these three people said that talked them out of a potentially disastrous problem but how they said it— their tones and the sincerity they conveyed. Conveying the right message along with the right tones can change many losing situations into winning ones.

VOCAL SELF-DEFENSE

Using the appropriate intonation, inflection, loudness, softness, emotional reaction, and body and face language can even save your life, as the following examples illustrate.

Jessica was a college junior who was at the university library one evening studying for an exam. It was about 11:30 P.M. and most of the people around her had gone home. She was engrossed in her books, oblivious to distractions.

All of a sudden she felt something on her ankle. She looked down and couldn't believe her eyes. There was a hand clasping her ankle. At first she was shocked but she quickly regained control. She took a breath in, tightened up her abdominal muscles, and boomed out as loud and as low as she could, drawing out her vowels, and feeling them resonate in her guts: "What can I do for you?" Immediately her would-be attacker scurried away, perhaps to find other prey who would sound and act more victim-like.

Many studies have been done about victims of crime. They found that those who walk victimlike, with the head down, a slow gait, and poor posture are more likely to be assaulted than those who project a more confident presence.

The same holds true for the tone of a person's voice. How you say things along with what you say can be the deciding factor in whether you live or die.

That tone doesn't always have to be forceful as in Jessica's case. It can be a soft, calming tone, depending on the situation you're in. It can save your life.

Alice walked into her dark apartment one night only to find

herself being told to take her clothes off by a would-be attacker who attempted to rape her. She was calm and conscious of her breathing. In soft, reassuring tones, she calmed her attacker down and talked him out of it.

In a calm, flowing tone she said, "Don't worry. I won't hurt you." This confused her attacker, allowing her to make a successful escape.

Sandra was alone in her office working late one night when she heard a noise in her outer office. She went into the room only to find a transient, a bum, who was all dirty and smelly. He looked disoriented. Although she was petrified and felt her heart racing as she kept her voice calm, she asked what she could do to help him. He said that he wanted to use the phone to call the moon. She calmly replied that her phone didn't make calls to the moon, but the one across the street did. She then scooted him out the door, locked it, and proceeded to call the police. Her smooth vocal tone not only calmed the bum but calmed her as well. She was able to keep her wits about her.

As unfortunate as it seems, the most important thing you need to be is mindful of all that is going on around you. Be aware! Notice people around you, especially in new buildings, garages, and elevators. Be aware and be alert in new places that can make you vulnerable.

In addition, be aware of situations that can make you vulnerable, such as asking for directions or the time, waiting for a bus or car, home deliveries of food or supplies, and home services (e.g., repairmen).

Vocal Tips to Deter Potential Attackers

1. Use confident body language when waiting for a cab or bus, or walking. Stand up straight, not hunched over or with head hanging down. Act like you know what you're doing and where you're going. Take longer steps, not little insecure steps. Be physically expansive and take up more space.

2. Look around you when you're walking or standing and don't let strangers invade your space. At all times, be aware of how close to you or how far away someone is.

3. If you are approached by a stranger, use deep forceful tones, squeezing your abdominal muscles for support in pushing them out.

4. Draw out your vowels when you speak. Doing so will make you sound more confident and more self-assured. Speak in short, direct statements. Use phrases like "Go away!" "No!" and "Stop it right there!" Your tone will often work for you. It's similar to the way animals respond to authority in a voice without understanding the words.

5. Practice opening up your vocal tube and pushing your tummy muscles down and out as you make the loudest tone you can. Really yell and project your sound until it resonates through your entire body. You need to practice this, especially if you're not the type of person used to loud vocalization.

6. When answering your door, use a strong, abdominally supported voice to ask who it is. If it's someone unexpected, ask, "What can we do for you?" Never admit you're alone. "We" gives the message that there's more than one person living there.

7. If you weren't expecting someone and you are alone, don't feel intimidated into opening the door. Tell the person to come back at a later time (tell him when) and that you are busy now. You don't have to feel obligated to let a deliveryperson you weren't expecting into your home. In a short command, you may want to say: "Leave it in front of my door." If you're unsure, it's better to sound rude and unwelcoming, as this can be a deterrent.

8. If you're asking someone for directions, never say, "Can you tell me how to get to Elm Street?" or "I can't seem to find Elm Street. Do you know where it is?" Never admit you are lost. You immediately become easy prey for a would-be attacker. Instead you may want to say, "Excuse me, what's the best way to Elm Street from here?"

9. Never ask the question, "Would you mind telling me what time it is?" Instead a more powerful statement would be either "What time is it?" or "What time do you have now?"

10. Look at the person eyeball to eyeball. Don't look up or down or shift your eyes from side to side. Direct eye contact

can give the impression of confidence and self-assurance. This will make the would-be attacker think twice before bothering you.

What to Do If You Are Victimized

When you are faced with an attacker, what usually happens? You freeze up and can't move due to shock. Rhythmic breathing basically stops, the wind is knocked out of you, and the adrenaline starts to flow. You can't speak, your voice goes up in a high-pitched, inaudible scream, or you aren't able to scream at all. If you are being victimized, the following tips should help you:

- Breathe! You need to oxygenate yourself. Take a breath in, hold it, and slowly let it out. This will help you get in control.
- Keep calm and stay cool. Jabbering and yelling can often frighten your attacker and make him or her more nervous. The attacker may end up doing something to you he wouldn't ordinarily do had you kept quiet.
- Try to keep your voice steady by supporting it through your stomach muscles.
- Only yell or scream to get attention if you feel the situation warrants it. Try to keep your wits about you, as difficult as it may seem.
- Don't get into any long philosophical or judgmental discussions at first. But once again, if the situation warrants it, keep talking to the person and use soft, gentle tones.

—6—
Nasality

NASAL WHINERS

Very few people like a nasal whiner. In fact most people are disturbed when they hear one. Our poll results show that close to 70 percent of people surveyed found a nasal voice one of the five most annoying talking habits. Listening to someone with a whiney voice can grate on your nerves so much that you don't even want to hear what that person has to say. People may even make unfair judgments about your intelligence or about your appearance if you sound nasal.

My doctoral dissertation shows that nasality relates to one's perceived attractiveness. In my study, I paired photographs of attractive-looking people, average-looking people, and facially deformed people with tape-recorded speech samples of normal voices, mildly nasal-sounding voices, and severely nasal voices. In pairing up all the different combinations of nasality patterns with facial attractiveness, I found that those subjects who were facially deformed but had no nasality were considered more physically attractive than they were when they had nasal speech. Conversely, the facially attractive subjects who had nasal speech were considered to be unattractive, even though they were previously judged to be physically attractive when they had non-nasal speech. This study clearly shows how the nasal quality of a person's voice can influence our judgment.

Unfortunately, nasal sounding voices seem to be epidemic in

our society. Research shows that we harbor the most disdain and prejudice against people who have this nasal whine. People with a whiney voice are usually the object of jokes and ridicule. Fortunately, most of the people who have this nasal whine are painfully aware of it. They have seen how poorly others react to them.

Perhaps the funniest illustration of this point was in Carl Reiner's movie *The Man With Two Brains*. Steve Martin rejects Randi Brooks, who plays a prostitute, because he is in love with a "brain." After his rejection, you hear Randi whining in a grating and comical nasal voice, "Why are you leaving? It's my voice, I know it's my voice!"

Remember the "whiners" on *Saturday Night Live?* It was hysterical to watch this family, who all talked with a nasal whine. We also laughed at comedienne Lily Tomlin's nasal, whiney character, the nosey Ernestine.

People in certain levels of society often sound nasal. I call them the "nasal lockjaw snobs." You know the type: people who take in an affected breath of air through their nose and tell you about Daddy buying them a new Porsche or having to run along or they will be late for the polo match. These people think they are the elite and would not dream of associating with anyone outside their circles. But the truth is that no one else would want to associate with them because they sound so annoying.

Unfortunately, the nasal whine is not limited to the "lockjaw snob," the "nasal princesses" have it too. These princesses are usually snobby and spoiled.

Francine Drescher, an excellent actress who sometimes plays "nasal princess" roles has starred in such films as *Saturday Night Fever, American Hot Wax, Doctor Detroit,* and *This Is Spinal Tap.* In each of these films, she played a character who has a nasal voice. The only problem was that in real life Francine continued to sound like the characters she played on screen.

Consequently, she was typecast. It was not until she got rid of her nasal whine that she opened up new dimensions in her acting career. She got numerous roles playing characters without a New York accent and a nasal whine. She now has an elegant non-nasal voice, but is still able to put on her nasal whine whenever a role calls for one.

Even though nasal whiners are funny on film and on stage, they are not so funny in real life.

Kathleen's case was almost tragic. Kathleen, an attractive, bright accountant got laughed out of every firm she applied to for a job. She had such a nasal voice that people thought she was joking or kidding around with them. She came to me to get rid of her nasality, wondering if she had some physical condition.

Two physical conditions that cause people to develop a nasal voice are a cleft or hole in the palate (roof of the mouth) and a short palate. These rare disorders can be treated with surgery or with prosthetic devices that fit into the mouth. Other people experience this nasal sound because of brain damage.

Kathleen had none of these problems. The roof of her mouth functioned perfectly and she had no nerve damage. Her problem was never opening her mouth when she spoke; she literally spoke through her nose. When she learned to use the techniques in this book to eliminate the nasal sound of her voice, she was amazed at how differently people reacted toward her. They seemed to treat her with more respect. She told me that her friends noticed the difference in her tones; they commented on how well she sounded when she spoke to them on the telephone.

Nasal whining appears to be a greater problem among women than it is among men. The results of the poll confirm this finding in terms of women's own perceptions of their voices. More women found a nasal whine offensive than men did. In fact, nearly twice as many women as men found a nasal voice to be annoying.

In order to tell if you are a nasal whiner, place your thumb and index finger on the bridge of your nose and say "Ba, ba, ba, ba." If you feel a vibration or buzzing in your nose as you say these syllables, you have a problem with sounding too nasal. You need to do two exercises, the Imaginary Dime Technique and the Jawing Exercise to help you get rid of your nasality. If you are not nasal, do these exercises anyway to keep from becoming nasal.

Actress Sela Ward (*Nothing In Common*) **demonstrates how to tell if you're a nasal whiner. She places her thumb and index finder on the bridge of her nose, and says "Ba, ba, ba." Sela is not a whiner; she didn't feel any vibration in her nose.** *Alan Shaffer*

The Imaginary Dime Technique

Most people are nasal because they do not open their jaws wide enough when they speak. They start out with open jaws, but clench down on their jaws as they proceed to speak, making them sound more and more nasal.

When you speak, pretend that you have an imaginary dime standing lengthwise between your back teeth, propping your jaws open.

Actually this is the normal position for your jaws to be in. When your jaws relax they automatically drop and your back teeth separate to a distance a dime standing lengthwise could fit into. Don't put any dimes in your mouth—you might swallow them. Remember, these are imaginary dimes, so just *pretend* that you have a dime propping open your jaws when you speak.

1. Keep your jaws propped open with the imaginary dime and make sure your back teeth are not touching.

2. Place your middle finger and thumb on the bridge of your nose.

3. Say, "Ba, ba, ba, ba."

4. Clench your jaws so that your back teeth touch.

5. Repeat steps 2 and 3 with your jaws clenched.

You should feel a difference between steps 1–3 and steps 4 and 5. In the first three steps you should not feel a nasal buzzing; in the last two steps, you should. If you feel a nasal buzz while doing steps 1–3, open your jaws wider and try again. If you still feel the buzz, you may want to get a medical examination by an ear, nose and throat physician to see if there is something wrong with the roof of your mouth. This exercise helps you feel the difference between when you sound nasal and when you do not.

You can see how important it is to open your jaws to avoid sounding nasal. The next time you speak to someone, make sure that an imaginary dime stands lengthwise between your

The photo on the left shows Dolph Lundgren demonstrating a clenched jaw, which makes so many of us sound nasal when we speak. The photo on the right shows Dolph demonstrating the Imaginary Dime Technique, in which you imagine a dime standing lengthwise between your back teeth propping open your jaws. *Firooz Zahedi*

teeth before you utter a sound. You will be amazed at how this technique will stop you from being a whiner. Remember that keeping your jaws together may be fine if you're a ventriloquist like Ronn Lucas, but it's not right for anyone else. The result is that you may end up sounding like a dummy.

Jawing Exercise

Jawing helps you open your jaws and get rid of the nasal tones. This exercise helps you learn how to talk using your mouth muscles and not your nose. It also helps you reduce mumbling by helping you open your jaws more. This technique is a modified version of one used in Europe by Dr. Emil Froeschels.

1. Open your jaws and pretend you are chewing out the following sounds:

    A. Yah—yah—yah ten times (do not be afraid if you feel your jaws cracking; just open your jaw wide and use your facial muscles).

    B. Next, do the same exercise with Yoo—yoo—yoo.

    C. Then with Ye—ye—ye.

2. Place a wad of gum in your mouth (forget for a moment what your mother taught you) and chew with your mouth open. Use the gum to cushion your teeth as you open your jaws and chew out the sounds that you did in 1 (A–C).

DENASALITY—CLOGGED UP NOSE

The other side of being too nasal is not being nasal enough or sounding like your nose is stuffed up.

Sometimes your adenoids are too big, or your sinuses are blocked, or you have another obstruction. If this is the case, you may hear "ba, ba, ba, ba" for "ma, ma, ma, ma." If this is the case, you need to have a checkup by a qualified ear, nose, and throat physician. The doctor will determine if you need surgery or medication to clear up your nasal obstruction. You will be surprised at the difference you will hear after you are treated.

I have seen Dr. Edward Kantor and Dr. Joseph Sugarman in Beverly Hills literally perform miracles for people who had these nasal obstructions. Their patients could breathe through their noses again after not being able to do so for most of their lives. So many people spend a good portion of their lives ignoring their nasal obstructions. When they finally do undergo treatment, their only regret is that they did not do it ten or twenty years earlier. So you do not have to suffer anymore. Get medical help.

How to Tell If You Are Denasal

To tell if you are denasal, do the following exercise: Place your thumb and middle finger across the bridge of your nose as you did when you were checking to see if you were nasal sounding, only this time say "ma, ma, ma, ma." You should feel a buzz in your nose as you say it, unlike the nasality exercise where you say "ba, ba, ba, ba." If you don't feel a buzz, you need to make an appointment with your ear, nose and throat physician immediately!

Resonation Exercises

The following exercises are designed to help you to resonate your tones. You should feel a lot of buzzing when you read.

1. In reading Robert Southey's "The Cataract of Lodore," whenever you see a slash mark, be sure to stop and take a breath in, hold it and then draw out the vowels as you resonate the tones.

/The cataract strong/then plunges along/striking and raging/as if a war waging/It's caverns and rocks among/rising and leaping/ sinking and creeping/swelling and sweeping/showering and springing/flying and flinging/writhing and ringing/eddying and whisking/spouting and frisking/turning and twisting/around and around/with endless rebound/Smiting and fighting/a sight to delight in/Confounding astounding/dizzying and deafening/the ear with its sound/Collecting projecting/and receding and speeding/ and shocking and rocking/and whizzing and hissing and/dripping and skipping/and hitting and splitting/and shining and quacking/and pouring and roaring/and waving and raving/and tossing and crossing/and flowing and going/and foaming and roaming/and dinning and spinning/and dropping and hopping/ and working and jerking/and guzzling and struggling/and heaving and cleaving/and moaning and groaning/and glittering and frittering/and gathering and feathering/and whitening and brightening/and quivering and shivering/and hurrying and scurrying/and thundering and floundering/and dividing and gliding and sliding/and falling and crawling and sprawling/and driving and riving and striving/and sprinkling and twinkling and wrinkling/and sounding and bounding and rounding/and bubbling and troubling and doubling/and grumbling and rumbling and tumbling/and chattering and battering and shattering/and retreating and beating and meeting and sheeting/and advancing and prancing and glancing and dancing/and recoiling and turmoiling and toiling and boiling/and gleaming and steaming and seaming and beaming/and rushing and flushing and brushing and gushing/and flapping and rapping and clapping and slapping/and curling and whirling and purling and twirling/and thumping and plumping and bumping and jumping/and dashing and flashing and splashing/sounds and motions forever/and ever are blending/all at once and all over/with a mighty uproar/and this way the water comes down at Lodore.

2. This exercise will help you feel even more nasal resonance. Say these sounds as rapidly as you can. Each sound should be said ten times in succession. Feel the buzz in your nose as you do this exercise.

Ma mo ma mo ma mo ma mo ma mo

After practicing these exercises, your nasal resonance will be richer and will sound better, not only to you but to others.

—7—
Diction and Pronunciation

SLOPPINESS IN PRONUNCIATION

The way you pronounce words can be a major factor in influencing people. Sloppy pronunciation, like leaving off "ings" at the ends of words (goin, doin, comin, instead of going, doing, coming), mumbling, and mispronouncing words, is a negative. Sixty-three percent of the people questioned in the poll found mispronunciation to be an annoying talking habit.

People who mispronounce words usually get an unfair reputation. Initially they're judged to be not very bright, especially if they mispronounce "r" sounds. The reason for this may be that so many mentally retarded people and deaf people have difficulty pronouncing "r" sounds that the same perception is carried over unconsciously.

Tina is an adorable seven-year-old who had difficulty pronouncing such sounds as "s" and "r." Her tears, when the other children on the playground told her that they couldn't understand what she was saying and refused to play with her, broke her mother's heart. She was withdrawn and painfully shy. The other children even resorted to teasing her and calling her names like "Mickey Mouth."

When she learned proper tongue placement for the particular sounds and words she had trouble with, she was able to make these sounds correctly. She is no longer teased and now has the confidence to make friends with other children.

Have you ever been so annoyed by people mumbling their words that you wanted to tell them to speak up or shut up?

Well, this kept happening to a client of mine. His mumbling speech was so annoying that you felt like there was a buzzing bee around you whenever you heard him speak.

Gordon became a millionaire by accident. He was a chemist who invented a product that earned him a lot of money and led him to employ a lot of people. He was not prepared for his new role. He had no interpersonal skills and no social life.

One of the reasons his social life was so terrible was that nobody could understand him when he talked to them.

After doing considerable work with Gordon on his image, his vocal skills, and, mostly, his pronunciation skills, he gained the confidence to meet new people.

One of the assignments I gave him was to meet five new people a day and begin conversations with them without mumbling. One of them was the woman he eventually married.

At his wedding he got up in front of five hundred people (most of them were his employees) and proposed a toast. This is something he never would have done before. People who hadn't seen Gordon for several years were shocked that he wasn't mumbling and that they could actually understand what he said during his toast.

People who lisp also experience a lot of prejudice. Research has shown that females who lisp are perceived as cute until they become adults. Then they are perceived as dumb. On the other hand, adult males who lisp are perceived as being homosexual. In many cases, this is true; a high percentage of gay men have developed a lisp as an affectation. I have treated a number of men, both gay and straight, who have come to me to help them get rid of their lisps so that they won't be perceived as being gay.

Whenever I'm on a call-in radio show, I usually get a call from someone asking me why so many gay men seem to sound alike. Why do they lisp and overpronounce words? My answer is that I don't know why they do, but it may be an affectation which makes them feel more a part of a certain social group. It may be like speaking Ebonics, or Black English, where one feels comfortable speaking the dialect with certain friends. The same is possibly true for gay males. In certain environments it may be fine; however, in the work force, it's not.

Mark, a gay man who had a severe lisp, wore an earring, and had a bunch of keys dangling from his pocket, worked for a large company. In the past two years he had noticed changes in the behavior of many of his coworkers toward him. Those women who previously were openly affectionate toward him would rarely touch him. Even though Mark did not have AIDS, he was still being treated like a leper by some of his coworkers just because he was openly gay. He came to me to help him with his image and with his speech so he wouldn't appear to be gay. After changing his style of dress to a more conservative look, taking off the earring and keys, and eliminating the lisp, he was able to get a new job. His new look and new speech pattern helped at his new job. His gayness is no longer an issue since it is no longer apparent in his dress or his speech pattern.

People mispronounce words for many different reasons. Although it is rare, some may have nervous problems which affect their tongue and lip placement. Some suffer from muscle laziness which results in mumbling. Others mispronounce sounds because of certain dental conditions. The vast majority of people mispronounce sounds for cultural reasons or because of foreign accents or dialects.

Most people mumble their words out of laziness and have underdeveloped facial and tongue muscles. Your talking muscles are just like the other muscles in your body. You need to work them out and use them in order to keep them in shape, as did Gordon, the Mumbling Millionaire. You need to open your jaws and use your tongue, lips, teeth, and throat to produce the correct sounds.

Sometimes the position of your teeth or the mobility of your tongue can contribute to problems with your pronunciation of certain sounds. Spaces between teeth, missing teeth, upper teeth that are protruding (buck teeth), lower teeth that protrude, crowded teeth, poorly fitting dentures, or new crowns all may contribute to the way you sound. If so, you need to contact a dentist (orthodontist or prosthodontist) as well as a speech pathologist.

Eugene, a stockbroker, spoke with teeth clenched together and mouth closed, making him mumble and making it difficult for him to be understood. His mumbling became such a problem that his clients repeatedly complained that they couldn't understand him.

After my first visit with Eugene, he revealed that he hardly opened his mouth when he spoke because he always hated his teeth and was self-conscious about them. He then saw Dr. Henry Yamada in Los Angeles, president of the Society of Aesthetic Dentistry, whose excellent artistic ability and use of acrylic bonding on Eugene's front teeth helped solve the speech problem. Not only did the dental work stop Eugene's mumbling, but the bonded teeth made him look great. He discovered that he had a sexy smile when he found more women acknowledging him with a smile.

CULTURAL MISPRONUNCIATION

Ebonics (Black English)

Most people who hear Ebonics, or Black English, feel that certain words are being mispronounced. Well, they are wrong. Ebonics is an accepted cultural form of communication. For example, "birthday" will be pronounced "birfday." The final consonant will be deleted. So the word "oldest" is pronounced "odes." The initial "th" sound in "this" and "that" is pronounced "dis" and "dat." The "l" or "r" sounds are left out, so "called" becomes "cawd" and "more" becomes "moe."

People who speak Ebonics are not mispronouncing words. Ebonics became an acceptable form of communication in 1974 when the Ann Arbor decision was handed down by the courts and teachers were told not to downgrade Black children. Even though Ebonics is considered to be a standard form of Black English which reflects the Black heritage and provides an extra bond among Blacks, it hasn't caught on in the business world.

Ten years later, in 1984, a study done by Drs. Sandra and Frances Terrill at North Texas State University found that blacks who spoke Ebonics received significantly fewer job interviews with fewer job opportunities and, if they were hired, received less pay than Black, non-Ebonic-speaking people. The results of this study have great implications in terms of the prejudice which still exists across this country with regard to Ebonics.

An interview I did with actor Dorian Harewood (*The Jesse Owens Story*) provided insight into the subject of Ebonics. Dorian grew up around people who spoke street language but also grew up with a mother and father who stressed that it was important to learn standard English because it was the language that would help him to succeed.

This facility of speaking both Ebonics and Standard English has helped Dorian Harewood immensely as an actor. He has gone from playing an Ebonics-speaking street gang leader to playing Simon Hayley on *Roots: The Next Generation,* who improved himself through his language and education so he could move up the ladder and participate in the American Dream.

Whenever possible, Dorian tries to educate Black youth by telling them they must learn to speak Standard English as well as Ebonics in order to have better success in life and open up greater opportunities.

A Black male attorney and a Black female gynecologist, whom I treat in my practice to help them incorporate more Standard English into their speech, both reported that they felt comfortable speaking Ebonics at home and with their friends but felt that they needed to de-Ebonicize their speech because they were being called upon to do more public speaking in predominantly White environments.

One of my clients whose diction I helped polish before he ventured into a new dimension of his career is Ben Vereen, now a popular television host and spokesperson. Ben not only had hints of Ebonics but a New York accent which resulted in "dis" and "dat" (this and that) and leaving off final "r" sounds.

Today Ben Vereen is one of the most sought-after television hosts. He is constantly asked to host shows all over the world because of his mass appeal.

Bill Cosby is another person whose non-Ebonic speech pattern breaks through all racial and social barriers, making him the nation's leading spokesperson. In fact, our Gallup poll shows that almost one hundred percent of the people questioned like the way he sounds, making him number one in the survey.

Most of the Blacks surveyed reported that they liked the Ebonic dialect little or not at all, while most of the Whites surveyed said that they liked Ebonics a lot or a little because of its ethnic flavor. The reason why most of the Blacks didn't like the Ebonic accent may be the prejudice they experienced as a result of speaking Ebonics, as Dr. Terrill's study pointed out.

Accents and Dialects

While watching the Fourth of July celebrations honoring the Statue of Liberty on television, I was moved by all of the interviews I saw with immigrants. These immigrants came to Ellis Island thirty and forty years ago from all over the world. I was impressed with each person's story and felt an emotional sense of pride as they spoke in their foreign accents. All three networks gave us the impression that we were all one and that it didn't matter where we came from or how we sounded. We were all Americans, united by the love of America. After watching these broadcasts, how could anyone ever feel prejudice again?

Well, the Fourth of July celebrations have long since passed and most people are back to being their old prejudiced selves, judging people by the way they look and even more by the way they sound.

Even though the survey showed that 75 percent of us are not irritated by the fact that a person has an accent or dialect, the way we feel about people's accents or dialects largely depends on what kind of accent they have and where they happen to be when they're using it.

Although a large number of Americans find a Southern drawl

charming, you had better not be drawling out your southern vowels for too long if you're asking someone for directions in New York City or you may never get there. You may not get people to listen to you. They may think you're too slow and leave you in mid-sentence.

By the same token, having a Brooklyn accent and barking out that you need to know how to get somewhere in Jackson, Mississippi, is likewise a problem. You may never be listened to. You too may be left in mid-sentence, as you may be perceived as being too pesky, demanding, and overbearing.

People do make judgments about your accent whether you like it or not. Sometimes, these judgments are accurate, as a classic British study by T. H. Pear done in 1931 points out. In an experiment he conducted with the aid of the BBC, he interviewed nine speakers of different ages, sexes, and interests over the radio. Prior to the experiment, he published instructions in a radio program magazine that included a form that listeners were to fill out and send in. He received over a thousand listener judgments about the nine speakers: ages, vocations, birthplaces, and places of residence. He also asked listeners to write a description of each speaker. With "surprising exactness" the listeners guessed the age, sex and vocation of the speaker. Later research has confirmed his findings. The socioeconomic status of Englishmen could be determined by their speech patterns.

Of course, this may be easier to do in England. Listen to the differences between the Cockney accent of the fabled Eliza Doolittle and the Queen's English of Professor Henry Higgins.

Besides judgments made about your socioeconomic status, judgments are made with regard to your intellectual status and your work abilities based on your accent. Several studies have shown that Mexican-American speakers are perceived more negatively with regard to their educational and occupational status than Anglo speakers are. Earl's case provides an example of how a particular accent can affect how people judge you intellectually. Earl's slow, sloppy Southern drawl played to the prejudices of his East Coast corporate clientele. They heard "lazy and unreliable" while, in fact, Earl was one of the most ambitious, hardworking people around.

Thomas, a psychology professor who had a Southern drawl, was on a panel with his student, who had an Oxford English accent. The audience directed more questions to the student even though the professor was the expert. The student, had an Oxford accent and appeared to be the expert, even though he wasn't.

So you see, we can harbor prejudices about our own accents because of the way other people treat us. As a matter of fact, only half of the Southerners questioned in the poll liked the way they sounded. One out of every three residents of the South disliked the way they sounded as compared to one out of every five residents of all other states. Perhaps these people were met with the same prejudices. It is unfortunate that so many Southerners feel negatively about their accents, because another survey I did showed that most people who are not from the South like the Southern accent and find it charming.

Finally, judgments are made about your personality characteristics based on your accent, as various studies have shown. Studies by Howard Giles at the University of Bristol in England and by Norman Markel and his colleagues at the University of Florida found that a regional dialect is a significant factor in judging personality characteristics from a person's voice.

Another study confirming these findings is an Australian study by Cynthia and Victor Gallois. They looked at the impressions Australian, British, French, Greek, and Italian accents had on Australians. They found that the British accent was rated most favorably and the Vietnamese accent least favorably in terms of personality characteristics.

Even though most of us generally don't mind a person having an accent, as the results of the following poll show, there are some accents that we like more than others.

I asked forty-one people between the ages of twelve and seventy-two, both male and female, if they like the following accents a lot, a little, or not at all. Even though the results of the study are not conclusive, there were apparent trends in people's answers. Twenty-five percent of the people tested had some type of accent. The rest had a standard American accent.

Here are the accents they were asked about and their answers:

	Like a Lot	Like a Little	Like Not at All
1. Arabic	4	12	25
2. Australian	32	7	2
3. Black English	6	10	25
4. Brooklyn	6	11	24
5. Canadian	12	26	3
6. Chinese	0	10	31
7. English	37	4	0
8. French	23	18	0
9. German	5	13	23
10. Greek	17	18	5
11. Hungarian	10	14	17
12. Indian	10	23	8
13. Iranian	3	6	35
14. Irish	27	9	5
15. Israeli	3	19	22
16. Italian	25	14	2
17. Jamaican	30	9	2
18. Japanese	3	17	21
19. Korean	2	11	28
20. Midwestern	4	22	15
21. New England	11	24	7
22. Portuguese	16	15	10
23. Russian	5	16	20
24. Scandinavian	28	12	1
25. Slavic	4	15	22
26. South African	18	8	15
27. Southern	22	12	7
28. Spanish	6	19	16
29. Valley Girl	2	3	36
30. Vietnamese	1	10	30

The ten accents that received the highest scores were: (1) English, (2) Australian, (3) Jamaican, (4) Scandinavian, (5) Irish, (6) Italian, (7) French, (8) Southern, (9) South African, and (10) Greek. The finding that most people favor an English accent is consistent with other studies conducted all over the world.

The ten least-liked accents were: (1) Valley Girl, (2) Iranian, (3) Vietnamese, (4) Chinese, (5) Korean, (6) Arabic, (7) Black

English, (8) Brooklyn, (9) German, and (10) Slavic.

The implications of this research are that if you have one of the accents that most people like, you may want to hang on to it because you won't meet up with many prejudices.

On the other hand, if you have one of the least liked accents, you may want to change it.

THEY MAY GET THE WRONG IDEA

Personally, I love accents and dialects. I love to hear the rich Latin accent of Ricardo Montalban, the sweet Southern drawl of Dolly Parton, and anyone with an English or British accent. I think that accents add a wonderful flavor to this country. However, accented speech can be a major problem if you can't understand what the person is saying.

Sometimes, using the wrong pronunciation in a particular accent can give an entirely different meaning. Numerous examples of this come to mind.

When I was working with Julio Iglesias on his award-winning song "To All The Girls," which he used to pronounce "Do Oll Dee Gelss," his Spanish accent was so thick that it might have been easy for listeners to misconstrue what Julio was singing. I was helping him with a phrase in one song—"Every breath that I take." Julio's accent made it sound like "Every breast that I take." With all the tabloid rumors about Julio as an international playboy, I didn't think that pronunciation would have been in Julio's best interest. You can see how important precise diction is if you don't want the meaning of something to be misconstrued.

Another example of someone misconstruing a word because of an accent happened when I was a guest on the Jim Eason radio talk show in San Francisco. A lady with a thick Cuban accent called in and in a machine gun tone asked, "Dr. Glass, wha' I ken du abow my espeesh?" I told her that she needed to slow down and draw out her vowels. She immediately jumped in and questioned, "My bowels?" Now, I'm sure she didn't even realize what she was saying.

Another case of misunderstanding happened to an American client of mine whose Chinese boyfriend wanted her to try a Chinese dessert he had prepared for her: "rokus." In disgust, his American girlfriend replied, "No way. I will never eat locusts. I'll throw up." He could only convince her after he wrote down the word "lotus", as in lotus flower. They both had a good laugh, and she ended up loving the dessert of lotus, not locusts.

It's important to correct your accent and dialect if you have too many embarrassing moments like the ones I've described, if people have a hard time understanding you, or if the accent makes you feel self-conscious. For example, several Iranian clients have come to me to reduce their accents because of the prejudice they were experiencing. They lost their self-consciousness about their speech, modifying their accents as they learned new ways to pronounce sounds.

YOU CAN LEARN ANY ACCENT

You might think that it is virtually impossible to change an accent or dialect. Well, it's not. Anyone can learn an accent.

If I can teach people how to acquire an accent, like Dolph Lundgren's Russian accent for *Rocky IV,* Conrad Bain and Dana Plato's Dutch accents for an episode of *Different Strokes,* and a variety of other actors who have had to play British, French, Hungarian, Polish, Italian, Czech, Cuban, and New York characters with their characteristic accents, it's easy for me to teach people how to lose an accent, depending, of course, on their motivation.

Dolph Lundgren lost his Swedish accent after three months. Sheena Easton was able to learn an American accent in about the same length of time. She is now able to use her native Scottish accent whenever she desires and is able to do a flawless American accent whenever a movie role calls for one. The key to loosing an accent is motivation. Both Dolph and Sheena were motivated because their future careers depended on it. You can study for ten years to lose your accent, but if you're not motivated, you'll never do it.

Why can't people lose accents even if they've lived in the United States for thirty years? Why is it easier for some people to learn an accent and not others? We don't know the answers to these questions, but there may be unconscious factors operating here. Perhaps they feel that the accent ties them to their past and their roots or gives them a unique identity. Other people may not take the time or have the interest to change their accents. They feel that learning English is just about all they are going to do. They already learned the language. Now learn the accent? Forget it!

Others block themselves by convincing themselves that they don't have an ear for accents. Others feel that they've gotten along with an accent and it hasn't gotten in their way, so why bother?

I say that you can learn to have any accent if you understand the melody, phrasing, consonant and vowel stress, and formation of a language. If you do, you will be on your way to losing your accent.

A big fear that people attempting to lose their accents have is that they will lose their past identity. Often, they will try to sabotage their progress when learning an accent. What they fail to realize is that changing an accent is not like changing your nose. If you don't like your nose job, it's hard to change back to your old nose. But if you don't like your new accentless speech pattern you can always go back to talking with your old accent. You can even use your accent with certain people and be accentless with others. You can choose to sound however you want to sound if you understand the basic phonetic rules.

When you're trying to get rid of your foreign accent and learn the new phonetic rules and ingrain these new sounds in your awareness, I recommend that you try to speak your native language as little as possible. However, don't go overboard! You can speak your native language if you have to. I repeat, you can speak your native language if you have to!

When treating Dolph Lundgren, star of *Rocky IV* and *Masters of the Universe,* to eliminate his Swedish accent, I neglected to tell him that he could speak Swedish if he had to. Because of his intense discipline and desire to eliminate his Swedish accent, he strictly followed my recommendations and did not speak Swedish even while he was in Sweden promoting his movie. He did a Swedish television show in which he was asked questions in Swedish. He was so accustomed to speaking English and doing his drills on his accent that he answered the questions in English. When the interviewer questioned him about this, he told the viewers that his speech and voice doctor in the United States told him not to speak Swedish. Yes, he was correct. I did tell him not to speak Swedish. but I should have added that it is quite all right to speak your native language if necessary.

WHY DO I MIMIC ACCENTS?

Why is it that whenever people are around other people with accents, they tend to mimic them? I meet so many Americans who tell me that they begin to use an English accent when speaking to an English person and they feel embarrassed by it. This also happens with Southerners. You may have never set foot in the South, but when you meet up with a Southern belle or Southern gentleman, you may find that you unconsciously copy their upward lilt or how they draw out their sounds. You may be embarrassed by this, especially if someone else points it out to you. You may feel that the other person may think you're mocking her.

Don't be embarrassed. This is a natural thing to do. You are mirroring other people's speech patterns either to make them more comfortable around you or to make yourself feel more comfortable around them. In most cases, the other person won't consciously notice what you're doing, but don't worry if he does. Most often, he'll be flattered.

If you do an accent well, you might even be able to use it to your advantage in a conscious way. I did that once when I was in a little Cuban dress shop in Miami. Because I asked about a dress using my Cuban accent, I got a discount, unlike my American-accented friend who bought a similar dress two days earlier for ten dollars more.

PROPER PRONUNCIATION EXERCISES

Many of us don't taste our words. We tend to mumble and fail to pronounce our words properly because we don't know how to position our tongue and teeth to produce proper sounds. The exercises in this chapter will help you with proper tongue, lip, and jaw placement for consonants and for vowel production.

Test Your Valves

The physical mechanism for the production of sounds is a long tube, our "speech tube," interrupted by a series of musculoskeletal valves (or pronunciation valves) at various locations, directed by the brain.

Matt Lattanzi (*Bill Crite*) **and Dolph Lundgren** (*Firooz Zahedi*) **demonstrate tongue and lip placement for the seven musculoskeletal valves:**

1. Bilabial valve (two lips together) for "p," "b," "m," and "w" sounds.

2. Labiodental valve (lower lip and upper teeth valve) for "f" and "v" sounds.

3. Linguadental valve (tongue tip out between teeth) for "th" sounds.

4. Lingua alveolar valve (tongue tip in back upper four teeth, both top and bottom) for "t," "d," "n," and "l" sounds.

5. Lingua palatal valve (tongue tip almost touching roof of mouth) for "sh," "j," "ch," "zh," and "r" sounds.

6. Lingua velar valve (back of tongue hitting back of throat) for "k," "q," and "ng" sounds.

7. Glottal valve (voice box valve) for "h" and vowel sounds.

A good way to tell if you are working the pronunciation valves properly is to say the following two sentences from the *Bloomer Mini-Test of Articulation 1973:*

1. We bought my father two new sunlamps.
2. You should choose a red coat hanger.

The sounds "w" (we), "b" (bought), and "m" (my) are made with the two lips together. The "f" (father) should be made with the upper teeth resting on the lower lip. The "th" in father should be made with the tongue between the teeth. "T" (two), "n" (new), "s" (sun), "l" (lamps) should be made with the tongue behind the upper teeth. "Y" (you), "sh" (should), "ch" (choose), "r" (red) should be made with the tongue against the roof of the mouth. "C" (coat) should be made with the tongue against the soft palate. The "h" (hanger) should be made with the back of the throat open.

Consonant Pronunciation: What to Do

The following exercises may help you with your consonant placement, as they exercise your muscles for speech:

   A. Bilabial (sounds made with the two lips together):

      ME MAY MY MO MU
      PE PAY PY PO PU
      BE BAY BY BO BU
      WE WAY WY WO WU

   B. Labiodental (upper teeth on lower lip):

      FE FAY FY FO FU
      VE VAY VY VO VU

   C. Linguadental (tongue between teeth):

      TH − (voiceless as in "think")
      THE THAY THY THO THU
      TH + (voiced as in "them")
      THE THAY THY THO THU

   D.1. Lingua alveolar (tongue tip against upper teeth):

      TEE TAY TY TO TU
      DEE DAY DY DO DU
      NEE NAY NY NO NU
      LEE LAY LY LO LU

   D.2. Lingua alveolar (tongue tip against lower teeth):

      SEE SAY SY SO SU
      ZEE ZAY ZY ZO ZU

   E. Lingua palatal (tongue against roof of mouth):

      CHE CHAY CHY CHO CHU
      JE JAY JY JO JU
      SHE SHAY SHY SHO SHU
      ZHE ZHAY ZHY ZHO ZHU
      RE RAY RY RO RU

   F. Lingua velar (tongue against soft palate or uvula):

      KE KAY KY KO KU

GE GAY GY GO GU
NGE NGAY NGY NGO NGU

G. Glottal (larynx or voice box):
HE HAY HY HO HOO

Besides tongue placement of consonant sounds, you may have difficulty with certain groups of sounds, such as *plosive* or air-producing sounds ("p," "t," "k," "b," "d," "g"), *fricative* or noise producing sounds ("f", "v," "ch," "j," "zh," "sh," "s," "z"), *nasal* sounds ("m," "n," "ng"), or *gliding* sounds ("l," "r").

Doing these exercises will help you to build up your speech muscles so that you will pronounce your sounds better.

A.1. Plosives
Say these sounds as rapidly as you can:
PPPPPP
BBBBBB
TTTTTT
DDDDDD
KKKKKK
GGGGGG

A.2. Plosives
Say these sentences as rapidly as you can:
1. Put the puppy on top.
2. Buy baby a blue bib.
3. Tim, the tiny turtle, ate.
4. Doggie didn't eat food.
5. Kate kicked the kitty cat.
6. Gary got a big egg.

B.1. Fricatives
Say these sounds as rapidly as you can:
FFFFFFFF
VVVVVVVV
SHSHSHSH
ZHZHZHZH
SSSSSSSS
CHCHCHCH
JJJJJJJJ

B.2. Fricatives

Say these sentences as rapidly as you can. Be sure to place the tongue tip against the lower teeth when saying "s" and "z" sounds.

1. Send his shoe measure to Charlie Jones.
2. Fifty-five fish were splashing.
3. The violets were over the glove.
4. She ate fish and washed dishes.
5. Zha Zha measured the room with pleasure.
6. He zapped the buzzing bees.
7. Sassy mice race across the ice.
8. Charlie will go to church after watching Chip do the chores.
9. Marge and Jan jogged along the edges.

C.1. Glides

Say these sounds as rapidly as you can:
WWWWWWWWWW
LLLLLLLLLL
RRRRRRRRRR

C.2. Glides

Say these sentences as rapidly as you can:
1. Woody wondered what the awkward crew would do.
2. Paul called the little lamb Lucy.
3. Ralph and Randy hurried across the river.

D.1. Nasals

Say these sounds as rapidly as you can:
MMMMMMMMMM
NNNNNNNNNN
NGNGNGNGNG

D.2. Nasals

Say these sentences as rapidly as you can:
1. Mary never sang.
2. Mom made Mona come home.
3. Nancy didn't send one to Don.
4. Mr. Chang was singing a song when the phone rang.

Vowel Pronunciation Exercises

Accents and dialects are often the result of manipulating certain vowels. The people who seem to be the most effective speakers tend to draw out their vowels.

There is something hypnotic about the rhetorical cadence set up by the repetitive sounding of vowels. Perhaps the ministers on television so captivate their audiences because they appreciate the vowel value in "speechifying."

Vowel sounds are produced by selective modification in the size and shape of the oral cavity or the oral portion of the vocal tube.

The vowel sounds of the American English language are: "e" as in beet, "ih" as in bit, "eh" as in let, "ah" as in bat, "aw" as

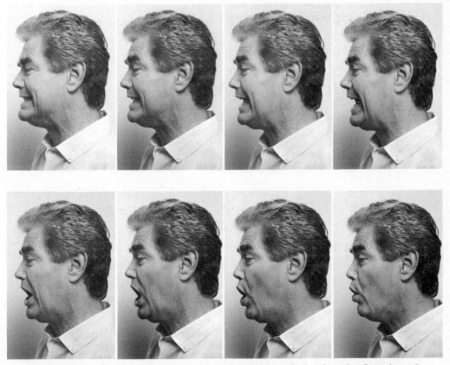

Joe Gallison shows the progressive dropping of the jaw in forming the vowels: "ee," "ih," "eh," "ah," "aw," "uh," "o," and "oo" vowel sounds.
Alan Shaffer

in bought, "uh" as in but, "o" as in boat, and "ooh" as in boot.

The following alliterative line can tell you a great deal about the way you produce your vowels: beet, bit, bet, bat, bought, boat, and boot. The most common error is between "i" and "e" as in "pin" and "pen." Watch your jaw open progressively as you say "ee," "ih," "eh," "ah," "uh," "oh," and "oo."

Repeat the following exercises. Be sure to draw out your vowel sounds when you do them. The exercises will help you with proper jaw placement. Be sure to say each of these words, going down each column in order, and notice how your jaw drops down little by little.

1. Say the following words and sounds, going down the columns.

PEEL	BEET	MEAT	EE
PILL	BIT	MIT	IH
PELL	BET	MET	EH
PAL	BAT	MAT	AH
PAWL	BOUGHT	MOTT	AW
PUHL	BUT	MUTT	UH
POLE	BOAT	MOAT	O
POOL	BOOT	MOOT	OO

2. Since discriminating the "eh" and "ih" sounds is the biggest problem in vowel production, doing these drills may be of some help to you. Go down the columns.

LID	LEAD	HIT	BET	HIM	BEN	LIN	LEN
MIT	MET	PIT	PET	PIN	PEN	HID	HEAD

3. The dipthong sounds in the American English language are: "o" (coke), "ay" (cake), "ow" (cow), "y" (kite), "oi" (coin), and "ew" (cue). Here are some dipthong drills for you to repeat and to help you with pronunciation. Go down the columns.

O	AY	OW	Y	OI	EW
COKE	CAKE	COW	KITE	COIN	CUE
NO	NAIL	NOW	NIGHT	NOISE	NEW
DON'T	DAY	DOWN	DIE	DOILY	DEW
BROKE	BRAID	BROWN	BRIGHT	BROIL	BREW

—8—
Clean Up the Way You Talk

In this chapter, you will learn some basic techniques to help you improve your grammar, enlarge your vocabulary, and reduce the number of filler words you use. We will also cover the topic of cursing and swearing—how people actually feel about it and when it's appropriate or inappropriate.

KILLER FILLERS: "LIKE UM, YOU KNOW"

Kevin, an insurance salesman, had an annoying habit that cost him thousands of dollars worth of business each year. His constant interjections of "like um," "and um" and "er um" made him sound tentative. He lost many potential clients. When he learned to control his "like um" and "and um" through the technique in this chapter, he sold many more insurance policies.

Another annoying filler is "you know." I remember hearing a lecture by a professor and counting twenty-five "you know"s during the first few minutes of the lecture. I couldn't concentrate on what he was trying to say but only focused on how many "you know"s I heard. I had no idea what the man was talking about because I was busy counting his "you know"s. During the break, I discovered that I was not alone. Almost everyone in the class was playing the same game. The game turned into a contest; we decided to guess how many "you know"s he would say before the end of the lecture.

Although this may seem mean or disrespectful, the professor's habit was so annoying that we could not help ourselves. It was either that or fall asleep. I regret, however, that no one stopped the professor during his lecture to let him know how annoying his "you know"s were and how difficult it was to concentrate on what he was saying.

Although it is a strict requirement for becoming a Valley Girl or Valley Dude, you don't have to use filler words such as "like um," "and um," and "you know." Many people who feel uncomfortable with dead space avoid silence by using these fillers. Don't feel uncomfortable—remember that at times "silence is golden." Don't feel compelled to fill the air waves with unwanted "like um" and "and um" interjections. Other people find them annoying. Close to 70 percent of the respondents in the poll confirmed this fact.

How to Kill the Fillers

1. Tape record yourself in different situations to monitor where and when you use the most fillers.

2. Play back the tape and count the number of times you use these filler words. You need to see how often you do before you can reduce and eventually eliminate this bad habit.

3. Substitute the "um," "and," "like," or filler word with a breath. Take in a breath for a second, hold it, and then begin to speak. This will help to control your use of filler words. Be patient but consistent at monitoring yourself and substituting the breath for the filler. The more you practice, the faster you will eliminate this problem.

IMPROPER GRAMMAR

People are intimidated by not having good grammatical skills. Only 22 percent of the people surveyed in a Roper Organization Poll felt that they were knowledgeable about their use of English grammar. Over 50 percent of the people surveyed felt that they were not taught enough about grammar when they were in school, while 81 percent felt that grammar should be given more attention. Even though such a small percentage of people feel secure about their grammatical skills, most of us feel that having proper skills is very important. In fact, over 86 percent of the two thousand people surveyed in the Roper Poll felt that using correct grammar creates a positive impression of a person. Our poll findings also confirm this as 63 percent of the respondents were annoyed by poor grammar. Most people perceive those who use proper grammar to be more intelligent and more successful than those who don't. Predictably, poor grammar and mispronunciation are more likely to offend college graduates than people without college experience.

Cheryl's case confirms this finding. Cheryl, an attractive twenty-one-year-old college student, uses "ain't got none" instead of "I don't have any," "I be" instead of "I was," and "I'm fixin' to go" instead of "I'm going." Many of her friends also use poor grammar when they speak, and therefore never correct her.

One day, Cheryl overheard two men talking about her while she was in a club. She had danced with one of them earlier in the evening and was on her way back from the restroom. One of them said, "The girl in that fuzzy red sweater is cute, but she's really a dumb bimbo—not too bright." Cheryl was devastated. She had hardly spoken to this man. How dare he conclude she was a "dumb bimbo" when he had spent only a few minutes talking with her! After all, he didn't even know her; but from the little he heard her say, he didn't need to know her better.

People hold horrible prejudices against those who use poor grammar. Unfortunately, judgments are made regarding intelligence, social status, and class. Obviously, all this man needed was a few minutes of conversation to reach the conclusion he did about Cheryl. Her poor grammar made him decide that she was not very smart.

Not using good grammar can definitely keep you from getting ahead socially, as well as professionally, as Cheryl's case clearly illustrates. I have many clients who have been passed over for promotions because of poor grammar.

Raymond worked in the repair department of a company

that sold office equipment. He wanted to be in the sales division of the company but was passed over for five years. This frustrated Raymond, and when he went to the head of the company to ask him why he was consistently passed over for a promotion, his boss said, "Raymond, I'd be embarrassed if you talked to anyone on behalf of our company. Your grammar is so atrocious that people might not take you seriously." He then told Raymond that he was not closing the door on him. If he improved his grammar and diction, he would be considered for promotion. Raymond came to see me and learned how to improve his grammatical skills as well as his diction. Today, I am proud to say, he is one of the top-grossing salesmen in the company.

Common Grammatical Errors

Even though we were taught subject-verb agreement, many of us have forgotten how to use the tenses (past, present, and future) properly. Even if you are well educated, you may be guilty of some of the most common grammatical errors:

(1) misused pronouns: I, me, him, her, she, he, us, we ("She got a card," not "from Ron and I," but "from Ron and me.")

(2) lack of agreement between nouns and verbs (Not "The boy and the girl jumps far," but "The boy and the girl jump far.")

(3) careless endings (gonna, shoulda, goin', woulda, comin')

(4) confused tenses and

(5) word and slang misuse ("she goes" instead of "she said")

Polishing Your Grammar

1. Open your ears and mind and listen to how other people put sentences together (using subjects, verbs and objects).

2. Get a basic high school grammar book and study it daily. Apply it to your conversation. Some dictionaries also have a section in the beginning that gives you some basic grammatical structures.

3. Eliminate "gonna," "wanna," "shoulda" in your speech; these are some of the most common errors.

4. Practice subject-verb agreement. ("The boy and the girl go to school," not "The boy and the girl goes to school.")

5. Pay attention to your tenses and keep them consistent.

Learning to use proper grammar won't take you that long. Almost all of us need to refresh our grammatical skills from time to time and to look up a grammatical rule that we are not sure about, so don't be embarrassed about doing it. Doing so can not only enhance how you come across but can make you feel more secure with what you want to say.

DO YOU HAVE AN ANEMIC VOCABULARY?

Have you ever been in a conversation with someone and suddenly felt uncomfortable because your vocabulary was not up to par? Have you ever wanted to express a thought but felt you didn't have the right words to express yourself? As many people as there are who feel insecure about their grammar, there are even more people who feel insecure about their vocabulary. Millions of people feel inadequate when it comes to expressing themselves in the right words.

Words are our tools for expressing our thoughts. If you don't have the right tools or words, how can you really get across what you mean? No wonder the divorce rate is so high. Words can make us laugh, cry, fight, or even fall in love. If your vocabulary is limited, so are your chances of success. One of the easiest and quickest ways to get ahead is to consistently build up your vocabulary.

The average adult has about ten thousand words in his repertoire, most of which he recognizes but never uses. So you can see just how much we are missing when it comes to expressing ourselves. Many people are embarrassed and even frustrated by this and think that there is nothing they can do about it. They feel that they are stuck!

Antonio, for instance, is a handsome Italian who came to live in the United States ten years ago. He has his own business, enough money, a beautiful home, a lovely family, and travels whenever he wants to.

Even though Antonio would be considered a success by American standards, deep down inside he felt as though he were a failure. He was insecure about his Italian accent, lack of formal education, and poor vocabulary. As a result, he didn't socialize much because he felt inferior and embarrassed.

He came to see me for help when two incidents happened to him in the span of a week. In one case, he didn't understand some big words used by a business contact. Antonio was too embarrassed to ask him what they meant. In the other case, his young son laughed at him because Antonio did not understand a particular word his son said.

Today, I am proud to report that even though he felt that there was nothing he could do, he now has a richer vocabulary and much less of an accent. His confidence is up and he feels more secure.

Like Antonio, Gale also felt embarrassed about her vocabulary. Gale was at a party where there were a lot of intellectual types in attendance. She felt the snobby airs put on about the room as she looked at these people engaged in conversations. They seemed to be in a world of their own.

Her boyfriend, Jim, introduced her to one of these "intellectuals," who kept spouting off big words. At times she wondered if he was speaking English. By this time she felt quite intimidated and decided to keep her mouth shut, not talking to anyone for the rest of the evening.

On their way home, Jim remarked at how quiet she was at the party and asked why she didn't talk to anyone. Immediately Gale started to cry, revealing her intimidation. She felt insecure because of her lack of vocabulary skills. She was afraid to open her mouth and let everyone know how dumb she was.

Fortunately, Jim was sensitive and could identify with her feelings. He suggested that she consult with me to help her develop her communications skills.

Gale is not alone in how she felt. Millions of people suffer from an anemic vocabulary which can hold them back in many areas of their life.

By increasing your own vocabulary, you may be increasing the vocabulary of those around you, especially your children and grandchildren. Remember Valspeak, the popular teenage slang? Valspeak shows us what a limited vocabulary teenagers have. To expand it, vocabulary building must begin in the home.

How to Learn More Words

You don't have to be a college graduate in English to have a good vocabulary. Anyone can learn new words and practice using them. Performer Ben Vereen puts it well when he says, "You never know how important words are until you have to communicate with the masses. Whether it's for the masses or in a personal situation, the more resources you have, the stronger the point you can make."

Before you begin to increase your vocabulary, it is important to remember not to get frustrated or discouraged. It is not done overnight. It is an ongoing process you need to work at constantly. Here's what you need to do.

1. Invest in a Tape or Book. To increase your vocabulary, buy yourself a vocabulary book or an audio cassette, such as my tape from Tape Data Media called "The World of Words," or use the dictionary regularly. Memorize three to five words a day and use those words in daily conversation.

2. Look It Up.

(A) If you come across a word you do not know while you are reading, write it down, look it up, memorize it, and try to use it in your own speech.

(B) Don't be afraid to ask what a word means or what a person means by what he said if he happens to use a word you aren't familiar with.

(C) Keep a list of new words and look at that list from time to time to refresh your memory. All of us can improve our vocabulary if we only do this regularly.

(D) Figure the word out from roots, prefixes, or suffixes. By studying Latin and Greek roots, which make up a large percentage of our language, you can easily figure out the meanings of many words.

(E) Figure out the word from its context. If you don't understand a particular word, try to figure out the meaning from the context in which it was said.

SLANG: WHAT ARE THEY TALKING ABOUT?

The meaning of words has changed so dramatically over the past few years that today's slang may be obsolete tomorrow. What was a "jerk" four years ago is a "nerd" by today's standards. What was "swell" in the fifties, "groovy" in the sixties, and "hot" in the seventies, is "awesome" in the eighties.

Remember when "cool" meant warmer than cold, "hot" meant the opposite of cold, "wicked" meant bad, "neat" meant organized, and "gay" meant happy? Well today, "cool" means hot, "hot" means cool, "wicked" means great, "neat" means wonderful, and "gay" means homosexual.

I think the funniest line in Burt Lancaster and Kirk Douglas's recent movie *Tough Guys* is when a beautiful girl asks Kirk Douglas, who has been released from prison after thirty years, if he is gay. With a straight face, Kirk replies "No, I'm not gay, I just lost my job."

Slang has been used by teenagers in almost every generation since the Mayflower, according to Stuart Berg Flexner, who wrote the *Dictionary of American Slang*. Slang is designed to keep adults out and give teenagers an identity of their own. For example, Valspeak, the San Fernando Valley phenomenon, was popularized by a fourteen-year-old girl's pop song, "Valley Girl."

To keep you abreast of some of the latest slang so you'll know what your teenager is talking about—at least this week—here are some general guidelines to let you know if what they are saying is favorable or unfavorable.

Favorable words are: "cool," "gnarly," "rad," "awesome," "babe," "fox," "bitchin'," "insane," "outrageous," "buf," "amped," "jazzed," "psyched," "stoked," "mega," and "far out."

Unfavorable words are "gross," "geek," "nerd," "turkey," "buzzed," "thrashed," "I'm sure," and "no way."

So even if you don't exactly know what these words mean, now you will know whether or not to smile when you hear any of them. It's also a good idea to learn the slang of the day and use it appropriately around teenagers. You may find that in doing so you will establish an even better rapport with them. Fer sure!

CURSING AND SWEARING

As liberal as we think we are, most of us are still offended by the use of profanity! In fact, the poll I took indicated that an overwhelming 84 percent of the respondents are offended by the use of profanity and find people who swear annoying. Over half of the people surveyed were annoyed a lot by swearing; it was the second highest ranked disturbing habit.

It is interesting to note that with regard to cursing and swearing the poll shows that there is a sex difference. Cursing annoyed over two thirds of the women (69 percent) a lot, while fewer than half the men (43 percent) found cursing objectionable to this degree. This has several implications, especially in terms of intimate relationships. A research survey I did for the Playboy Channel regarding what men and women talk about in the bedroom showed that most women were turned off by their mates talking dirty or using obscene language to them while lovemaking. Perhaps this is a point of contention in intimate relationships. Men need to know that most women don't like "dirty talk." If men become more sensitive to this, it may improve their relationships with women, not only in the boardroom but in the bedroom as well.

People do make judgments about you based on your use of profanity. Dr. Anthony Mulac at the University of California at Santa Barbara did an experiment to see if a speaker's use of obscene language affected a listener's attitude toward him. He found that those who used profanity were judged to be less social, less intellectual, and less attractive than those who did not use profanity.

Studies have shown that using profanity can affect your credibility. Those who use profanity are perceived as being less credible than those who do not. It can even cost you a job, as the research of Dr. Larry Powell and his colleague at the Mississippi State University showed. Their study showed that using profanity such as "son of a bitch," "shit," "damn," "asshole," or "fuck" in a job interview consistently made a negative impression on the interviewers and could obviously cost you a potential job. Your first reaction to Dr. Powell and his colleague's study might be, "Well, it's obvious, but I would never dream of using profanity during a job interview." On a conscious level this is true. However, if you use profanity frequently enough as part of your daily speech pattern, it may become a habit that is so ingrained in your subconscious that it might slip out.

This happened to a friend of mine who was doing a television talk show interview. He slipped and said some four-letter expletives. Luckily, the live broadcast was on a three second delay so they could bleep out his profane words. He did this about five times during the broadcast and was not even aware of it until he watched a tape of the show and heard all the bleeps. This certainly helped him become more aware of his cursing.

Just as having a good vocabulary can rub off and help improve the vocabularies of others around you, using obscene language can do the reverse. It can rub off on those around you and affect their total image as well.

One eight-year-old girl I worked with came into my office for her speech therapy session. After I asked her how her day was she told me that it was terrible because her teacher "got pissed" at her. Although it was rather funny to hear this child say that her teacher "got pissed" at her, it was also sad that she didn't even realize she was using a profane word which could affect people's perceptions of her. People may wonder what kind of a home she comes from. They may think that she comes from a low-class environment when in fact she doesn't. She merely thought "pissed" meant "upset" and it was OK to interchange the two.

Perhaps the most embarrassing incident I ever experienced was at a dinner party. A precocious three-and-a-half-year-old who was the son of the host and hostess kept getting out of bed and running downstairs in his pajamas to participate in the party. The mother tried to keep her cool and tried to explain to little Jordan why he couldn't be at the party, patiently telling him that it was a party for adults and not for children. He finally threw a temper tantrum and his mother proceeded to drag a wailing Jordan up the stairs. Everyone was silent as they heard his initial scream. Their silence turned into giggles and then into hysterical laughter as Jordan in all his anger called his mother a "shithead." His mother almost dropped him down the stairs; she has never heard him say this before. Many people at the party must have thought that precocious little Jordan must have picked up the word from his mom or dad. Although he didn't know exactly what the word meant, he did know that it is a word you are supposed to say when you're really angry and upset at someone.

So be especially careful in whose presence you use profanity, because it may come back to haunt you unexpectedly. On the other hand, profanity does have its place in certain situations. Swearing may be the only way you can possibly express your emotions. There is nothing wrong with that; for many, cursing is a wonderful tension releaser. Just be careful where and with whom you use it. In order to control your use of slang terms and curse words, which may prove to be embarrassing to you, there are three things you can do. Although it's difficult, these three steps have helped many people to reduce and eventually eliminate these words from their vocabulary.

1. The same technique that was used to get rid of filler words can be used in this case. Take a breath in, hold it and then let out air instead of the specific word you intended to use.

2. It's important to be mindful of the situation you are in and the person you are speaking with at all times. Imagine that you are an outsider observing yourself. This will help you avoid any potentially embarrassing situation.

3. Make a list of substitutions you can use for your pet slang and curse phrases. For example, if you constantly say "he's fulla shit," you may want to write down all of the phrases you can use instead—"he's full of it," or "he's full of himself," or "he's full of nonsense." If you constantly say "I'm turned on," you could write down "I'm thrilled with" or "I'm energized by." This technique takes only a few minutes to do and could save you many moments of embarrassment. Often we use profanity and slang because we can't think of any other word to say. If you have a repertoire of substitutions at the back of your mind, you'll never be at a loss for words.

—9—
How Do You Listen?

WE CAN'T STAND INTERRUPTERS

Almost all of us are annoyed by people who interrupt us when we are talking. The dramatic results of the Gallup poll bear this out: interrupting is the number one annoying habit! Close to 90 percent of the respondents reported that of all the annoying talking habits, interruptions annoy us the most.

Have you ever felt so frustrated by people constantly interrupting you and not allowing you to get a word in edgewise that you had visions of punching them the next time they interrupted you? How true the Bible verse that says: "He that keepeth his mouth keepeth his life."

When you interrupt other people and keep them from finishing their thoughts, you may elicit hostile behavior from them. So many arguments are initiated by not letting other people finish what they want to say. What may start out as a civil expression of points of view can end up in a heated brawl just because one of the parties is a poor listener.

We are a society of such poor listeners that we create unnecessary hostilities towards one another. We lose business contacts, friends, and lovers because we don't know how to listen.

Listening is a lot more than just hearing. When you hear

something, you just sense a message, but when you are listening, you are interpreting and analyzing what is being said.

Unfortunately, most of us just hear what we want to hear. We are not listening to what is actually said. The reason for this is that we are so busy thinking about what we are going to say next that we don't even bother to tune in and react appropriately to the other person. Most of the time we fly off the handle and verbally throttle the other person before we have gotten the whole message and know all the facts.

Linda, the wife of a newly appointed studio executive, wanted to buy a watch for her successful husband to enhance his image in his new position. He insisted that the family budget could not cover it, even though she knew how badly he wanted the watch.

She dropped the matter but several days later she saw the watch at a discount store for much less than the price of the one she had seen on trendy Rodeo Drive in Beverly Hills. So Linda purchased it.

Extremely excited, she said to her husband, "Remember that Rolex that we saw the other day?" Her husband angrily cut her off, shouting, "I don't want to hear another word about it. You know we can't afford it and that's that." He had not even bothered to listen. Had he bothered to learn all the facts, he might be wearing his new Rolex watch to his new job today. Unfortunately, his wife returned the watch the following day because she was so disgusted with her husband's reaction. I might also add that Linda is not perfect either. Instead of communicating with her husband, she ran away from the problem and sulked, pouted, and felt sorry for herself. She returned the gift out of anger. You not only have to listen but you have to communicate if you want your relationship to work and to keep working.

There are many warning messages in relationships that couples give one another that let them know just how the relationship is progressing. Unfortunately, many relationships fail because one of the parties didn't listen to all these messages. Grant, a forty-one-year-old stockbroker, should not have been so shocked and devastated when Carol, his live-in lover, took all of her belongings and moved out. For six months she had told him that she would leave if he didn't marry her at the end of the six months. She repeated her threat constantly during this period. When December came, Carol was out.

When Grant came in to see me for his appointment, he was white as a sheet and cried that he was a poor victim. How could Carol do this to him? She just got up and left. It was only after I reminded Grant that Carol had told him all along that she was leaving if he had no intention of marrying her that he regained his composure. Carol gave him an ultimatum and a time limit. When the time ran out and there was no marriage, she stuck to her guns and left.

Suddenly it was as though a light went off in Grant's head as he realized what a terrible listener he was. Carol had told him what she planned to do all along and he just didn't listen.

LISTEN TO WHAT OTHERS SAY ABOUT THEMSELVES

If you listen, you will know why things happen. Here is where mindfulness and self-awareness come into play. Really pay close attention to what people around you are saying, especially about themselves, and analyze how it relates to you.

When I was in college, we had a saying among the girls in the dormitory: "If a guy tells you he can be a jerk, listen to him. He's probably right." After all, who will know better than he. So often we go through life hearing what we want to hear instead of listening to what is really happening.

Judy, an average-looking Midwesterner, went out with Mike, a gorgeous East Coaster who was very popular. He wooed Judy, who by now was head over heels in love with him.

Judy was very complimentary to Mike but every time she would compliment him he would say, "Well, I'm not that great. You really don't know me. I can be a real shit."

Instead of putting her brakes on and looking at Mike's statement as a red flag, warning her of impending danger, she ignored him. Instead of asking Mike what he meant by his comment and how it could affect their relationship, she glossed it over, smiled, and said, "No, that's not true, you are so nice."

Well, Judy should have listened to Mike's assessment of himself because a week later he proved his point. He was a "shit." He dropped her without an explanation and would not return her calls, even after she accidently ran into him while he was walking arm in arm with another girl. She wished that she had listened to him so she wouldn't have gotten so emotionally involved.

We need to stop listening only to what we want to hear. We need to listen to everything that is said.

Because many companies have lost money due to human error largely because of employees' poor listening skills, many of the Fortune 500 companies throughout the United States have set up listening programs to teach executives how to listen to one another.

The military, the United States Senate, the Department of Labor, and the Army Office of Intelligence, among others, have also benefited from listening programs in helping to develop interpersonal relationships among employees. And even more important, listening programs have improved communications in critical job areas where crucial time was taken away from more important work.

Being a good listener can also be cost effective for your business.

WHAT IS A GOOD LISTENER?

Even if you are presently a terrible listener you can learn to become a good one. In doing so, you will not only improve your interpersonal relationships but business relationships as well.

A good listener is someone who takes advantage of what he or she can learn and respond to and does not let his/her mind wander. A good listener must remain focused on what is being said and doesn't make judgments until after the speaker is finished talking. This is perhaps the most difficult thing to do. For so many of us it is a supreme effort not to jump in and vomit out our opinions. We need to let the other person finish speaking, and we need to stop interrupting.

I encourage people to do the In Hold Out technique (take

a breath in through the mouth for three seconds, hold it for three seconds and then proceed to speak) in order to help them become better listeners. The few seconds it takes to take the breath in and hold it before you speak gives the impression that you have digested what the other person was saying, because you have taken time instead of jumping in and responding. Doing this gives you time to open your ears and your mind to what the other person is saying.

One of my good friends, Dr. Paul Cantalupo, a Beverly Hills psychoanalyst and psychiatrist, has a great saying about listening that one of his patients taught him and that I always keep in mind, especially when I work with clients. He says that "God gave us two ears and one mouth so that we can listen twice as much as we talk." What a great thing to keep in mind, especially if we want to improve our interpersonal relationships with people. Everyone loves a good listener!

The next time you get together for dinner with friends, or see an old friend, or even make a new one, ask them about themselves and then practice the listening rules which follow in this chapter. You may not only be surprised at what you will learn but you may notice things that you never noticed before. You may also be surprised at how much better they will relate to you. I suggest this to couples who are fixed up for dates and nervous about meeting for the very first time. It works quite well because they learn more about the other person in a relatively short period of time.

I recently attended a Halloween party with a friend of mine at Joe and Melissa Gallison's home. Joe is the star of the soap opera *Days of Our Lives*. At the party, I met a man, a writer, who I thought was one of the nicest men I had ever met, and whom I would love to run into again. The friend I was with also had a chance to talk to this man at the party. While driving back from the party, my friend and I discovered that we both liked being with the writer. It suddenly dawned on us that the reason we were both so taken with this man was because he was such a terrific listener. He asked us many questions about ourselves and kept his attention focused on each of us individually. He made my friend and me feel as though we were the only people at the party. No one else seemed to matter as he focused on what we said. Whenever we finished saying something, he would summarize it and ask another provocative question based on something he had tuned into in our last statement.

He hardly talked about himself except to expand upon a point we had made. For example, when I told him that I worked with people's speaking voices, he told me that he has always been fascinated by the quality of people's voices—that whenever he writes, he makes sure to include a description of how his characters' voices sound, whether the character has a high-pitched shrill voice or a low bass voice. He then jumped into another question concerning my work. This man never interrupted me and always let me finish what I wanted to say. He appeared to care and to be so genuinely interested in what I did and what I said that when I left him, I was feeling important and good about myself. My friend felt the same way and I am convinced that this writer is as successful as he is because of his wonderful ability to really listen.

In order to feel that you are having a great conversation with someone, both of you have to be good listeners. It requires both parties to employ the listening skill rules, not just one party. It is a give-and-take situation, and one has to be sensitive to the other person's body language, as well as take cues from him based on what he is saying.

Listening is a question-and-answer game that stimulates us, unlike the following joke that is circulating around Hollywood: An actor meets someone at a party and continues talking about himself and bragging about all the roles he is up for and how terrific he is. He goes on and on and doesn't pay any attention to what the other person is saying. He doesn't even look at the other person, for that matter. He is too busy seeing who just walked into the room, searching for a contact who could be more helpful to him in his career. After an hour of his ego-centric, self-absorbed conversation, the actor turns to the person he is talking to, looks right into that person's eyes and says, "Now, enough about me! Let's talk about you! What do you think of me?" Although this scene is comical, it's unfortunately all too true.

BECOME A GOOD LISTENER

You need to memorize the following four rules and exercise them whenever you meet someone new. Practice them regularly. If you do so you will be a lot more popular on the social front and a lot more successful on the business front.

1. Be mindful. Focus on what other people are saying instead of focusing on yourself and only talk about yourself as it relates to a point they make.

2. Maintain eye contact or face contact. Stop looking around the room. It is so disconcerting and makes the other person feel unimportant.

3. Do the In Hold Out technique when listening. Take a breath in through the nose for three seconds, hold it for three seconds and then let it out through the nose for six seconds as you digest what the other person is saying. Doing this, especially after you are asked a question, not only allows you to digest the information and formulate what you are going to say, but it also gives you the physical appearance of having listened.

4. Don't interrupt or cut off, especially when you hear an emotionally laden word, or a word that may push your buttons, like "racism," "God," or "sex." Let them finish what they are saying so that you get the entire message, then jump in. Cutting other people off makes them feel hostile. This in turn can make you feel hostile, which starts a vicious circle of anger instead of an exchange of beliefs and information.

—10—
How to Talk to Yourself

So far, we have seen the importance of cleaning up the way you talk so that others will feel better about you. It is equally important to clean up the way you talk to yourself so that you will feel even better about yourself. In turn, people will feel better about you because of the confidence you project. This chapter will show you how to have more positive self-talk by mirror techniques and by getting to know yourself better through a Getting to Know You survey.

You may not think that your negative self-talk holds you back, but it does. It feeds into the insecurities that stop you from pushing ahead in life.

STOP SAYING NASTY THINGS TO YOURSELF

Most of us are mean to ourselves. We constantly tell ourselves that we are not good enough. We tell ourselves how dumb we are, how stupid we are, that we forgot to do this or forgot to do that. We do it so often that we begin to believe it! In fact, it's like what the prophets have said in the Bible, "What things you say and believe in your heart all come to pass," and negative things continue to happen to us.

How many times can you recall yourself saying, "Oh I'm so dumb" or, "How stupid of me" or, "What a dumb thing I did" or, "That's my luck, it figures."

How many times can you remember looking at your tired face in the mirror after getting up from a restless night and saying, "Ugh, I look terrible!" or, "My hair looks awful" or, "My skin is disgusting, look at all these lines, look at all these zits." By giving yourself these negative little jabs, you are using negative self-talk, convincing yourself that you're not worth being liked.

You may very well have terrible skin and look awful, but you can break it to yourself gently. "Let's see what I can do to look better today" is a far cry from what you probably say.

Your constant barrage of verbal self-abuse and negative self-talk can do a lot of damage to others' perceptions of you. This can cost you a great deal, in personal relationships as well as in job opportunities.

Heather, a client of mine who was an actress in commercials, was one of the most physically gorgeous women you could ever see. She had perfect facial features, a terrific body, and dressed beautifully. She looked as though she had it all. Unfortunately, she did not have the positive self-talk to go along with her looks. Whenever I would compliment Heather on her makeup and clothing and tell her how great she looked, her reply was programmed as follows: She would not say thank you, but would look in the mirror, fluff up her hair, and say, "I don't look that great. My hair—(fluff, fluff)—I hate my hair. It's so awful, it's so thin."

I couldn't see anything wrong with Heather's hair, but she would always verbally beat herself up about it. Once I even told her how well she was doing with her speech and how her great new voice would match her terrific looks. This compliment didn't even faze Heather. In her ritualistic manner, she looked in the mirror, tousled and fluffed up her hair, and said, "Thanks, but my hair, I hate my hair." This went on so often that I stopped complimenting Heather all together, for fear I would hear about her hair.

One evening I happened to be at a party. Heather was at the

same party. I happened to be standing near a number of prominent casting agents who cast people in television commercials. Heather walked by and said hello to them and then left. When she was out of hearing range, I overheard one of the casting agents say to another, "What about Heather? She might be right for the commercial you're casting." The other agent replied, "Nah, her hair's too thin and too messed-up."

I couldn't believe what I had just heard. Heather put out so much negative self-talk about her hair that other people began to believe it, so much so that they felt her hair would be a problem if they hired her to do a commercial.

I can assure you that Heather's hair was normal, but even if she really did have a problem with her hair, she needed to stop verbally abusing herself and do something about it.

Our negative self-talk can allow people to see things about us that are not there. I remember once glancing at one of the tabloids. The headline was, "Christie Brinkley Thinks She Has Fat Thighs." They had a photograph of Christie in a bathing suit and I remember examining the photograph and thinking to myself, "Yeah, she does have heavy thighs," but if the headlines had read, "Christie Brinkley Thinks She Has Great Thighs," I probably would have looked at the photo and thought, "Yeah, she does have great thighs. What an inspiration! I need to do some more leg lifts at the gym."

We tend to see and hear what other people tell us about themselves. After all, who knows better than they do?

We think that we are sounding humble and unconceited when we cut ourselves down with negative self-talk, but in reality we are making a terrible impression on ourselves as well as on others.

The negative public relations we put out reaps negative public relations from others. You don't have to say "I'm so great" to everyone you meet, but you need to put across some self-confidence.

Muhammad Ali told us he was great. He knew he was the greatest before we did, and he was. He put out positive public relations about himself and we bought it. He complimented himself (why not!) and we followed.

There is a female star in Hollywood who could be a superstar but may never be because of her negative self-talk. Whenever she is on a major talk show, she puts herself down. She may think that she is being humble, but what she doesn't realize is that most people don't want to hear about how terrible she thinks she is. Nobody wants to hear all of her insecurities on television. We begin to question her work even though we have enjoyed watching her movies in the past. The next time we see her perform, many of us will probably doubt her abilities as an actress. If I were a producer, I would never give this woman any work, unless it was a role for an insecure woman with a poor self-image, because if she doesn't think she is good, why should anyone else? After all, who knows more about her abilities than she does?

How did all of this negative self-talk begin? How did we start to become so mean to ourselves? Much of it has to do with the conditioning we received in our society as children.

How many of us were told not to get too bigheaded or not to think that we were so great? When we were three years old, parading around in our crisp new party dress, or in our shorts and bow tie, saying, "Look at me," our parents made a big fuss about us. They told us how precious and adorable we were. Anything we painted or any new words we said were considered to be wonderful and brilliant. Our grandparents, the neighbors, our aunts, uncles, cousins and anyone else who would listen were told about the brilliant things we said and did.

But when we were ten and twelve years old, this all stopped. Why did we all of a sudden become uncute and unadorable and unbrilliant? We were told to stop being a show-off or were even ignored when we paraded around in our new clothes. We labored over drawings only to get an "oh that's nice, by the way did you make your bed?" We were told not to be so full of ourselves or so conceited when we reiterated to our parents what they had told us all our lives: that we were cute and adorable.

Pieces of healthy self-esteem have been chipped away without our even realizing it. We have heard so much verbal abuse while growing up that as adults we continue where our parents and teachers left off. This is why it is so important to talk to your children with respect so that they will learn to talk to themselves with respect. Of course this is hard to do sometimes, but children have feelings too! You would be surprised at the damage your verbal abuse may cause later on. I have done a great deal of work with parents in my private practice, teaching them to use positive self-talk with their children. The parents are amazed at how well this technique works and how much better their children behave and listen to them. The nicer you talk to yourself, the less tolerance you have for people who don't talk nicely to you, and the more quickly you will make it known that the way they are talking to you is unacceptable.

Often people will try to stand in your way. They will "rain on your parade" or "pop your balloon." Don't listen to these people. If you listen to all the negative voices telling you that you will never make it, you will be nowhere tomorrow.

How often, while doing my doctorate, did I hear that there is no such area of study as speech and genetic diseases and who did I think I was to embark on this new area that did not exist? Now, at the American Speech, Language, and Hearing Association conventions, seminars in this area are given regularly.

I never listened to the negative voices that told me I could not open a private clinic on my own, and in Beverly Hills yet, nor be on television regularly, nor become a personality, nor write a book or a movie script.

Why? Because I know who I am. I knew that I could do it. I had the self-confidence to work with the best. I envisioned myself treating celebrities, corporate executives, bank presidents, and politicians. I knew I had something special to offer and went for it. Don't let any of the "energy vampires" or negative voices infect you. Get rid of them.

In order to feel better about yourself and continue feeling good about yourself, you need to surround yourself with people who talk positively to you.

Get rid of Mary, who always has a snide remark when you tell her something good about yourself or what exciting things you are planning to do. The next time she says, "Well, just be careful and don't get your hopes up" after you told her that you just got fixed up with a gorgeous young neurologist, let Mary go.

Whenever you tell Gary about a new idea you have, he never fails to put in his two cents and offer advice even though you didn't ask for it. Instead of sounding pleased and perhaps asking if he could offer some additional help or insight, he makes you feel as though you are mentally retarded. If this happens all the time, you certainly don't need Gary's friendship, especially if you feel that he is always berating you and verbally tearing you down.

You need to be around people who speak lovingly and positively to you, even if they are giving you advice or telling you things you aren't too thrilled to hear. The key is how they say it! Remember, a pat on the back is only a few vertebrae removed from a kick in the butt. You can tell how much a person cares about you and respects you by how they talk to you!

In order to get rid of all the people around you who don't support you in your greatness, blow them out emotionally and physically. Blow out all ties you have to them and keep them out of your life. They are "energy vampires." Use the Tension Blow-Out exercise and blow them out of your life.

Just because you have known Nancy or Kevin since you were six, don't feel you still need to keep them in your life if they are not contributing to it.

Periodically, look at your Rolodex or private telephone book and make mental notes of those people who don't make you feel good about yourself—those who say insulting things to your face or behind your back. Ask yourself if you really need these people in your life. We need mutually satisfying and supportive relationships in which we give positive talk and get positive talk back. Perhaps the best illustration of this is a true story about a gorilla named Koko who could communicate with humans via sign language.

Koko received a pet kitten as a gift. They became fast friends and communicated beautifully with one another. They would play together and the kitten would sleep curled up in Koko's arms.

One day the kitten escaped through the cage and was killed by a car. This saddened Koko greatly.

To ease his depression, Koko's trainers brought him another kitten. But he couldn't communicate with that particular kitten. It would jump around the cage, run away from Koko, and wouldn't cuddle up with him.

Koko asked his owners to keep bringing him kittens. Finally Koko found the right kitten, one that not only allowed him to be nurturing and communicative but that nurtured and communicated back. We can learn a great deal about surrounding ourselves with positive influences by Koko's experience.

"SAY NICE THINGS IN THE MIRROR" TECHNIQUE

One of the most terrific clients I ever had was an incredibly successful businessman from Texas named Wayne, whom I met after I gave a lecture to his company. Wayne was a self-made multimillionaire with a great attitude. I saw how his positive self-talk helped make him the success he was. He told me that every morning, after he woke up, he would look into the mirror and talk to himself.

With his upbeat and positive attitude and his enthusiastic energy, he would wish himself a good morning and say: "Good morning, Wayne. It is good to see you. We are going to have a terrific day and all kinds of great things are going to happen to us. We are going to have fun and make a lot of money today! Right? You bet!"

You probably think that Wayne is crazy or at best that this is a corny or dumb thing to do. But how dumb can it be? Wayne is making millions of dollars a year and gives himself a pep talk every morning before he makes all that money, so it obviously works for him. Now, I'm not saying that if you use this positive self-talk technique and say great things to yourself in the mirror every morning, you will make a million dollars, but who knows? You just might!

If you positively program yourself and your day, who knows what you may attract—a good relationship, more money, a better sex life? You never know.

I must admit that I have tried Wayne's technique and it does seem to have a positive effect on how I begin each day. I feel great after doing it, and I am sure that I project this positive attitude on to my clients and on to other people I do business with. This in turn brings in more money, more people, more adventure, and more fun, which makes me feel more positive when I wake up and start the cycle all over again, beginning with my positive self-talk.

Who knows what comes first, the positive experiences which generate the positive self-talk or the positive self-talk which generates the positive experiences? Who cares? All I know is that it works for me and for many of my clients. I tell them to do it for two weeks and to see what happens.

Most of them resist it and think that it is insane to talk to one's self in the mirror. Well, they soon come to find out that it is not insane and that it does work.

One of my clients, Cara, a thirty-eight-year-old single attorney, used the positive self-talk technique to program herself to be more receptive to finding a man she could marry. For the

Actor and model Bob Beck (the Camel cigarette man) does the Positive Self-Talk Technique in the mirror. *Bill Crite*

first week she was discouraged and felt that the technique was a waste of time. I encouraged her to keep doing it, which she reluctantly did. The second week, she started doing more things to expand her ability to meet eligible men. By the third week she had two dates. A month later (the fourth week), she was infatuated with the man of her dreams, whom she met while having lunch with a client. The fifth week he asked her out. By the sixth week she had a date with a different man each night, including her dream man. By the tenth week, she was dating her dream man exclusively, and a year later, she married him.

I am not guaranteeing that this will happen to everyone, but it did work for Wayne and for Cara and it may work for you too. Just program what you want to happen to yourself and verbalize it positively. Mean it, and say it with all the conviction you have, and see what happens. It is certainly worth a try.

A COMPLIMENT? WHY, THANK YOU!

Most of us are so unfamiliar with talking nicely and positively to ourselves that when someone else does, we are taken aback. We don't know what to say or what to do if someone compliments us.

In my seminars and workshops, I ask people to give the person sitting next to them a compliment. I watch a lot of uncomfortable people squirm and their faces turn red as they blush.

Why is it that you can't tell people openly how you feel about them? It certainly would make for a better world if you did, but most of us have never learned how. We've been trained to think that it is OK to not build ourselves up and not react to those who build us up, either. What warped values!

The way you receive and give a compliment says so much about you as a person. When you really are able to love yourself, other people react differently to you.

The reason the commercial agent remembered Heather's hair was that every time he complimented her, she wouldn't acknowledge the compliment. She proceeded to put the agent on the defensive by verbally abusing her hair. In essence, she made the agent question his own perceptions of her, which subsequently cost her a job.

When you receive a compliment graciously, you not only feel better, but you make the person who gave you the compliment feel better. If someone compliments what you are wearing, say "Thank you. I really appreciate your noticing what I have on." That is so much more positive than "Oh, this old thing."

Think of how you feel when someone answers, "You're crazy" or, "You're kidding" after you go out of your way to tell them how good they look.

By acknowledging compliments, you are acknowledging yourself. Graciously accepting positive feedback and contributing additional positive feedback not only enhances how you feel about yourself, but how the person giving you the compliment feels about you. Besides, he or she will feel free to send out more compliments in your direction, which will start the cycle of positive feeling all over again.

Be careful of backhanded compliments. Do NOT accept them!

Sarah was giving a workshop in Seattle and found a penny on her way into her limousine. She said, "Well, this is a lucky day. I found a penny for good luck!" All of a sudden, a woman to whose group Sarah was speaking said, in a very sarcastic tone, "Oh, that's my penny. I dropped it but you go ahead and keep it, because you have to talk and you'll need it more than I will."

Had the woman said the following, she would have left a better impression in Sarah's mind: "Oh, that's my penny. I dropped it but you go ahead and keep it, because it will bring you good luck today."

Unfortunately, many of us have to hear barbs and jabs from people around us. We really don't need to let these people influence how we feel about ourselves.

Do not accept these negative comments. Reject them! Throw these comments back to the person who gave them to you. Ask them to explain themselves, indicating your nonacceptance. This will often make them think about it again. It will let them know that you will not accept negative talk from anyone.

TO KNOW YOU IS TO LIKE YOU

Most of us use negative self-talk and say bad things about ourselves because we don't know ourselves very well. Without ever thinking about it, most of you can fire off what your best friend likes to eat or wear, what his favorite color is, what he likes to do for fun, and what movies he likes to see. But if you asked yourself the same questions, you would have to stop and think for a while.

To learn more about yourself, fill out the following Getting to Know You survey. Write down the first answer that comes into your head. You will be surprised at how you see yourself.

There are no right or wrong answers. The answers merely provide you with a profile of how you view yourself. If you learn more about yourself, you may learn to accept more things about yourself, learn to like yourself better, and in turn speak more positively to yourself.

Getting to Know You Survey

Favorite color_____
Favorite type of music_____
Favorite movies_____
Favorite actors and actresses_____
Biggest turn ons_____
Biggest turn offs_____
Favorite books_____
Favorite animal and three adjectives describing it_____

_____
Favorite bird and three adjectives describing it_____

_____
Biggest fantasy_____
Males you admire_____
Females you admire_____
Favorite season_____
Favorite sport_____
Type of clothes you like best_____
Three things you like best_____
Three things you love to do for fun_____

If you were on a desert island, name three people you would want with you_____
If you were on this island, what foods would you want?_____
Favorite place to visit_____
Favorite place to live_____
Favorite car_____
If you could own one luxury item, what would it be?_____
_____

If there was a disaster and you could only take one thing with you, what would it be?_____
My biggest fears are_____
Handsome men make me feel_____
Beautiful women make me feel_____
The two men I love the most are_____
The two women I love the most are_____
What upsets me the most is_____
What makes me laugh is_____
The best thing about me is_____
The worst thing about me is_____
What makes me cry is_____
I could vomit if_____
When I get angry, I_____
When I am attracted to another person, I_____
Whenever I am nervous, I_____
I see myself as_____
Others see me as_____
Next week, I want to_____
Next month, I want to_____
Next year, I want to_____
In the next five years, I want to_____
Create a special place for yourself (a very special place, anywhere you choose). Decorate it._____
_____
_____

Furnish it. What is outside? What does the inside look like? What does the outside look like? How do you feel in it? What do you do when you are there? Who is there with you? What do you feel like when you are there?_____
_____
_____
_____

I am: (Write down a list of adjectives describing everything you feel you are.)_____
_____

What is the good news about you?_____
_____

What is the bad news about you?_____
_____

What things can you do to get rid of the bad news about you?_____

There are so many items in the survey that help you learn more about who you are. If you analyze the survey, you may find that you have more interests than you ever thought.

Now that you know "you" a lot better, you can be a lot nicer to yourself. If you left blank spaces or couldn't answer certain questions, you may want to work on developing those parts of yourself a little more.

You should fill out the questionnaire periodically to assess how your interests have changed and how much you have grown as a person. Do it every three months (Spring, Summer, Fall, Winter) to get the best results. It is a good way of measuring how well you know "you" throughout the seasons of the year.

–11–
Exercise Summary

You've done all the exercises in the book and you've had fun doing them, but you worry that the program could take forever to do. Well don't worry anymore! The program is simple and only takes about ten to fifteen minutes to do each day. You can do the exercises when you wake up, while you're preparing breakfast, or even while you're driving to work. You can also do these exercises throughout the day—whenever you think of them.

Here is a simple routine that you can follow to help you create a better sounding image.

The first step in preparing for the exercises is to make sure you're relaxed. There are a number of exercises to help you relax. These exercises also help you become more aware of your posture, your facial muscles, and breath support.

1. Head Rolls: Slowly rotate the head to the right, back around to the left, and forward. Do this five times, beginning at the right, and reverse five times, beginning at the left.

2. Shoulder Rolls: Rotate your right shoulder forward and leave it there for three seconds. Rotate your left shoulder forward, leaving it there for three seconds so that both of your

shoulders are forward. Next, rotate your right shoulder back and then your left shoulder back so that both shoulders are back. Repeat this exercise ten times.

3. Facial Relaxation: Close your eyes. Then consciously relax your forehead, eyebrows, eyes, cheeks, nose, lips, jaws, ears, and neck, concentrating on each facial part for approximately five seconds. For the next twenty seconds, visualize your faraway relaxing fantasies.

4. Relaxation Breathing: Put one hand on your upper chest and the other on your stomach. Take a breath in for three seconds and hold it, keeping your upper chest down, expanding only your tummy muscles. Exhale all the air and feel your tummy muscles contract. Do this five times, making sure you do it slowly and gently.

Now that you're relaxed, you need to open up your vocal tract and project in order to produce rich, flowing tones.

5. Sustained Football Player Voice Technique: Open the back of your throat as you inhale for three seconds and immediately exhale, producing a low, deep sound like that of a football player. Do this five times.

6. Ka-Ga-Ha: Say "Ka-ga-ha" in succession for as many times as you can until you're out of breath. Remember to open up the back of your throat and push your tummy muscles down and out to project the tone. Do this five times.

7. Chair Pushes: Place your hands on the arms of a chair (or on a steering wheel) and gently push down as you exhale, making the "ah" sound for as long as you can. Remember to open up the back of your throat as you feel the bouncing tone in your tummy. Do this five times.

8. Chair Pulls: Do the same things that you did for the chair pushes, only this time gently push up as you exhale the "ah" sound. Do this five times.

9. Ha-Ha Tummy Bounces: Take a breath in, opening the back of your throat and immediately exhale, saying ten Ha-has. Feel the sounds bouncing in your tummy.

Sometimes your pitch can be too high or too low, or your tones can be monotonous and boring. These exercises help you to excite your vocal cords.

10. Up-Down Glide Technique: Say the vowel "ah" and move up the scale for two notes above your OPL, holding each note for three seconds. Then take a breath in, hold it, and move down the scale for two notes below the OPL. Finally, glide up the scale without stopping at each note as high as you can go comfortably. Next, glide down the scale as low as you can go comfortably.

Here are some exercises to help you with your pronunciation:

11. Consonant Exercises: Say each one of the following sounds as fast as you can for as long as you can on a single breath.
P   F   TH   T
S   K   H

12. Vowel Exercises: Say the following vowels in progression, dropping your jaw farther for each vowel sound. Be sure to exaggerate the vowel sound and the opening of the jaw.
EE   IH   EH   AH
AW   UH   O   OO

The following exercises help you get rid of nasality and resonate your tones so you don't sound nasal:

13. Jawing Exercise: Drop your jaws and exaggerate chewing out the tones:
YA   YOO   YE

14. Nasal Resonance Exercise: Say "MA, MA, . . . " for as long as you can on one breath. Feel the buzzing sound in your nose, lips, and sinus cavities.

Now that you've made all these sounds, you can make even more pleasant sounds when you do the following:

15. Mirror Technique: Look in the mirror. Start by saying "hello" to yourself in the most energetic voice possible. Be sure to smile. Keep talking to yourself out loud, saying only good things to yourself. For example, tell yourself about all the good things you're going to make happen today and how good you're going to feel doing them. If you find that you don't like something about yourself, talk to yourself about how you're going to change it. Remember not to say anything negative. Build yourself up as you would a best friend.

These exercises only summarize the entire program. If you want further details for a specific problem area, be sure to go back to the appropriate chapter in the book. Remember that this book is also a reference book to be used whenever you need a shot or a boost of self-confidence.

Remember, doing the fifteen summary exercises only takes from ten to fifteen minutes. If you do them, you will be on your way to having great talking habits that won't annoy but that, instead, people will enjoy!

Have fun and a better sounding vocal image to you!

Where to Get
More Information

If you would like more information about videotapes, audio-tapes, lectures, professional counseling, or Vocal-Robics™ wear, fill out this form, enclose a self-addressed, stamped envelope, and mail to:

Your Total Image, Inc.
c/o Dr. Lillian Glass
435 N. Bedford Drive, Suite 209
Beverly Hills, CA 90210
(310) 274-0528

Name_____
Address_____
City, State, and Zip_____
Telephone Number (Area Code_____) _____

Please send me more information on:
_____Videotapes
_____Audio tapes
_____Lectures to companies
_____Private sessions
_____Group sessions
_____Workshops
_____Vocal-Robics™ wear

Index

About the Author

Dr. Lillian Glass is recognized as one of the world's foremost authorities on communications skills and self-image. In addition to having a successful private practice in Beverly Hills, California, she is a media personality.

A former professor at the University of Southern California Department of the Arts and Sciences, and Schools of Medicine and Dentistry, Dr. Glass earned her bachelor's degree in speech and hearing sciences from Bradley University, her master's degree in speech pathology from the University of Michigan, and obtained her doctorate in communication disorders from the University of Minnesota.

She also did postdoctoral work at the University of California, Los Angeles School of Medicine, Department of Pediatrics, and was awarded a fellowship in medical genetics.

Her lectures and published work have established her as an expert on speech and hearing problems arising from genetic and psychological disorders.

She has treated children and adults with facial deformities, including "little people" in whom inhibited growth also causes problems in communication.

Independent of her busy practice, Dr. Glass served as a communications specialist and health reporter for the Los Angeles ABC affiliate KABC-TV *Eyewitness News* for several years. Her "Total Image" segments not only offered viewers tips for communicating more effectively, but also offered them rewarding information on how to feel better about themselves.

Additional work in front of the camera has included co-hosting several talk shows, such as *Alive and Well* and *A.M. San*

Francisco. She has appeared on *The Today Show, The Merv Griffin Show, Hour Magazine,* and many other television and radio programs across the United States and throughout the world.

As well as being a media personality, Dr. Glass has coached many celebrities on their voices, accents, and dialects. She herself is an expert dialectician and can imitate dialects from all over the world.

Some of her celebrity clients include: Dustin Hoffman, Julio Iglesias, Ana Alicia, Conrad Bain, Bob Beck (the Camel cigarette man), Barbie Benton, Rita Coolidge, Jamie Lee Curtis, Bob Cummings, Donna Dixon, Don Diamont, Alex Donnelly, Fran Dresher, Sheena Easton, Barbara Edwards, Joe Gallison, Melanie Griffith, Dorian Harewood, Jeffrey Kramer, Robert Lamm, Matt Lattanzi, Gloria Loring, Rob Lowe, Ronn Lucas, Dolph Lundgren, Debra Sue Maffett, Tracy Nelson, Sarah Purcell, Bob Rafelson, Ben Vereen, Herve Villechaize, and Sela Ward.

She has also worked with several sports figures, including professional golfers and members of the Los Angeles Lakers basketball team and the Los Angeles Raiders football team.

Her expertise has been invaluable to corporate executives, politicians, and the general public in improving their image through their voice and communications skills.

Dr. Glass and her work have been the subject of important features in such publications as *The Washington Post, The New York Times, USA Today,* the *Los Angeles Times,* the *Los Angeles Herald-Examiner, Vogue, TV Guide, Los Angeles* magazine, *Cosmopolitan, Glamour, Self, Seventeen,* and *Success.*

On a much lighter note, Dr. Glass wrote *How to Deprogram Your Valley Girl,* which received national attention. She also has a top-selling audio tape called *World of Words.*

Dr. Glass's technical articles have appeared in numerous publications and professional journals. As one of the foremost authorities in her field, she has lectured throughout the world and is currently on the Board of Directors of the National Association of Hearing and Speech Action, a Washington, D.C.-based consumer advocacy group for the speech and hearing impaired.

OTHER BOOKS OF INTEREST

Say It...Right by Lillian Glass, Ph.D. 0-399-51699-9/$12.95
A guide to exactly what to say in almost any business or social situation.
A Perigee Trade Paperback

Doing What You Love, Loving What You Do
by Dr. Robert Anthony 0-425-12738-9/$12.00
A Berkley Trade Paperback

Finding Your Niche: A Handbook for Entrepreneurs
by Laurence J. Pino 0-425-14148-9/$9.00 *A Berkley Trade Paperback*

Get the Job You Want in 30 Days (Revised Edition)
by Gary Joseph Grappo 0-425-13961-1/$12.00
A Berkley Trade Paperback

Making a Difference: Twelve Qualities That Make You a Leader by
Sheila Murray Bethel 0-425-12309-X/$12.95
A Berkley Trade Paperback

The 10 Commandments of Business and How to Break Them
by Bill Fromm 0-425-13216-1/$7.95
A Berkley Trade Paperback

True Success: A New Philosophy of Excellence
by Tom Morris, Ph.D. 0-425-14615-4/$14.00
A Berkley Trade Paperback

Fishy Business: How the Wisdom of the Angler Can Help You Succeed
at Work by Jim and Bill Ignizio 0-425-16018-1/$12.00
A Berkley Trade Paperback

The Heart of Conflict: From the Boardroom to the Bedroom, to the
Battlefield, Understanding the Paradox of Conflict as a Path to Wisdom &
Harmony by Brian Muldoon 0-399-51824-X/$14.00
A Perigee Trade Paperback

On the Market: Surviving the Academic Job Search
Edited by Christina Boufis and Victoria C. Olsen 1-57322-626-2/$12.95
A Riverhead Trade Paperback

1,001 Ways to Market Yourself and Your Small Business
by Lisa Shaw 0-399-52314-6/$12.95
A Perigee Trade Paperback

TO ORDER CALL: 1-800-788-6262, ext. 1. Refer to Ad #586

The Berkley Publishing Group
A member of Penguin Putnam Inc.
200 Madison Avenue
New York, NY 10016

*Prices subject to change

OTHER BOOKS OF INTEREST

The Way of the Leader by Donald G. Krause 0-399-52267-0/$12.00

For centuries, great leaders have followed the theories of Sun Tzu and Confucius to win victories through effective use of leadership power. Now the author reinterprets these leadership principles for the modern businessperson working in today's volatile economic climate. *A Perigee Trade Paperback*

The Art of War for Executives
by Donald G. Krause 0-399-51902-5/$12.00

Sun Tzu's 2,500-year-old Chinese text, *The Art of War*—with advice on leadership, strategy, competition and cooperation—is adapted to modern business practices.   *A Perigee Trade Paperback*

The Adventure of Leadership
by Hap Klopp with Brian Tarcy 0-425-14376-7/$10.00

"Hap Klopp provides all the right reasons to break out of the corporate embalming fluid and take on the adventure of leadership." —Harvey MacKay *A Berkley Trade Paperback*

Deming Management Method
by Mary Walton 0-399-55000-3/$13.00

W. Edwards Deming, the genius who revitalized Japanese industry, offers his revolutionary system for overhauling American management. *A Perigee Trade Paperback*

Deming Management at Work
by Mary Walton 0-399-51685-9/$13.00

Practical applications of the highly acclaimed Deming Management Method. *A Perigee Trade Paperback*

Not for Bread Alone by Konosuke Matsushita 0-425-14133-0/$12.00

From one of the century's most accomplished business leaders comes a unique and profoundly thoughtful approach to financial and personal achievement.   *A Berkley Trade Paperback*

The One Minute Manager® by Kenneth Blanchard, Ph.D., and Spencer Johnson, M.D. 0-425-09847-8/$9.95

The runaway #1 international bestseller that has taught millions how to simplify their lives, get more done in less time, and find peace of mind.   *A Berkley Trade Paperback*

Putting the One Minute Manager® to Work
by Kenneth Blanchard, Ph.D., and Robert Lorber, Ph.D 0-425-10425-7/$10.00

The essential follow-up to the phenomenal success program that took the nation by storm.   *A Berkley Trade Paperback*

TO ORDER CALL: 1-800-788-6262, ext. 1, Refer to Ad #585

The Berkley Publishing Group
A member of Penguin Putnam Inc.
200 Madison Avenue
New York, NY 10016

*Prices subject to change